Class 58

Life & Times Series

Class 58

Colin J. Marsden

Oxford Publishing Co.

Introduction and Acknowledgements

Although currently the most recently introduced BR main line diesel class, the now 50 strong fleet of Co-Co Class 58s are some of the most popular locomotives in traffic today.

Designed by BR at Derby and constructed by BREL at Doncaster the Class 58s were introduced due to the increased need for purpose built Railfreight motive power, following the resurgence of railborne freight traffic in the mid 1970s. The Class 58 was a follow-on to the Class 56 Railfreight locomotive introduced quickly in the 1970s to fulfil a gap in the traction fleet, following projected increases in MGR and bulk load traffic. However, this design was little more than an updated Class 47. Whilst adequate this did not fulfil the projected requirement and the design office at Derby was given the job of producing detailed plans of a low cost, modular machine that would, with minor modification, be suitable for the export market, and at the same time be competitive alongside European and American designs.

Plans for the new generation modular Railfreight locomotive were finalised in 1978 and work commenced at Doncaster on the first example in 1979. The initial order was for 35 machines, but a follow-up contract eventually led to the fleet of 50 we see today. To coincide with the launch of the first locomotive in December 1982 the Railfreight sector introduced a new livery and logo to improve their image. This scheme of grey body with wrap round yellow ends was the standard livery applied to all the build, but with the new sector ownership and dedicated traction fleets introduced in 1987, they are now emerging in a revised livery.

After their initial testing, concentrated at Doncaster and from the Railway Technical Centre at Derby, the entire Class has been allocated to the country's largest diesel depot at Toton near Nottingham. From there the fleet, as will be seen through the pages of this book, operate over a wide area, ranging from Northfleet on the Southern Region, to Garston, Immingham and York.

Unfortunately BR's projection that the Class 58 design, or a derivative, would fair favourably on the export market fell by the wayside. This was not for the want of trying, as many delegates visited the works, and observed the locomotives in traffic, but competition was fierce. Indeed, when BR accepted privately owned traction for its tracks in 1985, the Foster Yeoman stone company favoured the American General Motors JT26CW-SS type (BR Class 59) in preference to any British unit available.

After the 50th BR example of the Class 58 had been constructed the jigs and assembly equipment were scrapped, ensuring that no further production would be possible.

Although fitted with electronic wheel slip/slide protection equipment, the Class 58s have always suffered from prolonged slipping on arduous rail conditions, particularly in colliery areas. This problem was highlighted with the sophisticated slip/slide protection equipment fitted onto the Class 59s, which virtually eliminated the problem and as an indirect consequence the final Class 58, No. 58050 was fitted with separately excited (SEP-EX) traction motors, together with other electronic equipment supplied by Brush.

At the time of writing in January 1988 no major problem or serious accident has befallen the fleet, and after the anticipated teething troubles of any new locomotive, they have settled down to return of an 80% availability figure over a twelve month period. This may well be significantly increased with the new maintenance policy now under way and it is anticipated that the Class 58 design will survive well into the 21st century, with projected withdrawals around the year 2015.

One of the most difficult operations involved in the production of this book, has been to break up the seemingly endless procession of Class 58s on MGR trains, as in all fairness, whilst associated with the movement of coal, the machines do operate other consists, although on a slightly infrequent basis. This book attempts to bring together a collection of illustrations of these superb locomotives on a cross section of duties.

The production of this book, the first in a major new series, would not have been possible without the invaluable assistance of BREL staff at Doncaster, especially Mr. E. Marshall and Mr. D. Porter who provided facilities to photograph the construction of the locomotives, and a special 'thank you' must go to these gentlemen. I would also like to record my sincere thanks to the many photographers who have assisted with material, especially Mr. John Tuffs, who has provided a considerable number of illustrations and much information on Midland workings. The final note of thanks must go to the publishers who have granted me complete freedom in the content and layout of this title.

If any reader wishes to further their knowledge and follow the Class 58s, there is a very active 'Class 58 Locomotive Group' who regularly visit railway establishments around the country, as well as providing an informative bi-monthly magazine. For membership details reference should be made to regular advertisements in the popular railway press.

Colin J Marsden
Dawlish

A FOULIS-OPC Railway Book

Published by:
Haynes Publishing Group
Sparkford, Near Yeovil, Somerset. BA22 7JJ

Haynes Publications Inc.
861 Lawrence Drive, Newbury Park, California 91320, USA

British Library Cataloguing in Publication Data
Marsden, Colin J.
    Class 58.
    1. Great Britain. Railway services:
    British Rail. Class 58 diesel-electric
    locomotives
    I. Title   II. Series
    625.2'662'0941

    ISBN 0-86093-422-5

Contents

Half title page: Before entry into service No. 58042 was displayed at the then BREL Doncaster Works mini open-day held on 3rd May 1986. This illustration, taken the previous evening, shows the locomotive sharing paint shop yard space with preserved Class 55 'Deltic' No. D9000.

Colin J. Marsden

Frontispiece: With the enormous cooling towers of CEGB Didcot Power Station towering above, No. 58011 is dwarfed as it departs with empty HAA hoppers bound for one of the Midland pits on 27th March 1985.

Colin J. Marsden

The major stamping ground for the Class 58s is the Erewash Valley line, stretching north from Toton to the abundance of NCB pits in the area. After slight overnight snow, No. 58023 passes the site of the long closed Ilkeston Junction station on 18th February 1985 with the 15.40 Toton Yard to Silverhill Colliery.

Colin J. Marsden

Development

Class 58 development can be traced back for many years, to 1973 when the British Railways Board (BRB) were informed that the rapidly escalating oil prices indicated a major growth in the movement of coal, and potentially an upsurge in general freight traffic, particularly in the field of block train consignments.

Until this time the BRB policy had been towards mixed traffic (passenger/freight) locomotive types. However this policy would not be desirable if vast tonnes of freight were required for movement. With some 80% of its motive power being more than 10 years old the railways of Britain faced something of a dilemma as most of their power was unsuitable for heavy, long distance freight movement, while the timescale advised gave little or no time to develop and test a new 'freight only' design.

Such was the urgency for the new freight motive power that BR invited tenders from British, European, and American builders for new or off the shelf designs based on a broad BR specification. After only minor deliberations an interesting British based tender was accepted for the construction of 60 locomotives jointly by BR and Brush Electrical Machines (BEM). The Brush involvement was such that their British undertaking developed the plans and effected design work, while the construction of the first 30 locomotives was carried out under licence by Electroputere of Romania, who were then able to offer the design for sale to other Eastern Bloc countries. The remaining locomotives of the order were to be constructed by BREL at Doncaster. These locomotives classified by BR as 56 were basically an updated and uprated Class 47 locomotive, but did not offer any specific advantages over existing types. Therefore the Class 56 project, while extending to 135 locomotives was only considered by BR as an interim design until 'new generation' purpose-designed freight motive power could be developed. It was envisaged that considerable savings could be made in construction costs if modular building practises were followed in place of the monocoque principles, and it was also felt that if a modular design was formulated where various large 'parts' were bolted to a common frame member, much time could be saved in maintenance and in particular if collisions occurred.

Whilst the Class 56 build was being carried out a considerable amount of design work was being effected on the new standard freight locomotive, and during 1978 BR projected that if a modular 'standard' locomotive design was established, a saving of 14% could be made in construction costs, and 16% in classified maintenance costs, based on 1978 figures. By early 1979 the decision was taken to develop the new purpose built freight locomotive, which was then given the classification 58, Doncaster Works being awarded the constructional contract, where work commenced late in 1979.

For many years the most common sight at the head of the HAA or merry-go-round coal train was the Class 47, their demise coming after the Class 56 build came on stream, following BR's decision to invest in purpose-built freight motive power. On 10th September 1981 Class 47 No. 47216, now renumbered to 47299, passes Stainforth & Hatfield with an empty HAA train.

Colin J. Marsden

Although the Class 56s were introduced from Spring 1977, the motive power position was still far from settled, as the Class was virtually an updated Class 47 with slightly more power. Hauling a loaded 32 vehicle rake of HAA wagons Class 56 No. 56074 *Kellingley Colliery* passes Doncaster station on 31st August 1981.

Colin J. Marsden

Following the decision to invest in new purpose designed Railfreight motive power, much of the projected equipment had to be tested, Class 47 No. 47601 which had previously been used to test Class 56 equipment, was further rebuilt to evaluate a Class 58 power unit and associated equipment, the locomotive emerging from BREL Crewe Works in 1980 as No. 47901. It was initially allocated to the ER, and latterly to the WR. No. 47901 is illustrated passing Berkley, near Frome with a stone train bound for Merehead Quarry.

Colin J. Marsden

Much of the equipment to be installed in the Class 58 locomotives was previously untried on locomotive designs, so a number of trials had to be carried out in the course of development work. Probably the most significant was the testing of the new Ruston-Paxman 12RK3ACT power unit, the first of which was delivered to BR in 1979 and fitted by BREL Crewe into Class 47 No. 47601, which had previously been used to test 'new' equipments used in the Class 56 build. When installed with its new 12-cylinder power unit and alternator group the Class 47 was renumbered 47901 and placed in service on the WR, always at the head of freight traffic where continuous observation could be given. Bogies for the standard freight locomotive were again to be of a totally new design, classified CP3 and fabricated by BREL Crewe. For development of these, Class 56 No. 56042 was fitted with a similar CP1 design bogie when new for evaluation work, a 'test' bogie was also given thorough strain and fatigue tests by BR Research at the Railway Technical Centre, Derby.

When the BR standard freight locomotive was first designed it was envisaged that there was considerable export potential as a number of railway companies throughout the world could benefit from modular constructed traction. A number of design options would be available on any export model, such as a single cab, vacuum train braking, or regauging to any specification between metre and 5 ft gauge. Regrettably, although many foreign railway administrations viewed the Class 58s under construction and in traffic, no firm orders were placed. This is a very great shame as in locomotive design and operational fields it was considered the Class 58 had much to offer, and stood up well against European and American competition.

The bogies intended for the new generation freight power were classified CP3, and constructed by BREL Crewe. To enable structure and stress tests to be carried out before the first locomotive was completed, the first finished bogie was transferred to the Research Division at Derby, and is seen in this illustration under strain tests. Note that pressure can be applied from overhead hydraulic packs to simulate differing body weights.

Colin J. Marsden

Design and Building

During 1977, BREL utilised the services of BR's Locomotive Design Office at Derby to prepare a report and feasibility study for a 'new' generation, low-cost Co-Co freight locomotive which would be suitable for both home and export markets. The resulting design was based on a simple underframe, formed of rolled steel joists, with a non-load bearing superstructure. This offered the required financial savings compared with the high-cost monocoque-bodied Class 56, which was basically an 'off the shelf' design. The 'new' design was soon accepted by the BRB as the low-cost standard freight locomotive design. Subsequently it was decided that after the completion of 135 Class 56 locomotives, all resources would be placed on the purpose-designed freight locomotive by now classified as Class 58. The Class 58 was essentially an attempt to match lower construction costs, and better maintenance features with the basic specification and power equipment fitted to the Class 56s, which had been successfully proven in arduous traffic conditions.

Some of the first cuts of steel plate, which eventually led to locomotive No. 58001 were made during Spring 1981, when parts of the frame members were cut and welded, following assembly of 'works' jigs. In this illustration the first top frame member for a spring pocket is seen on the Butler milling machine.

Derek Porter

The front end of the Class 58 model does differ slightly from the finished product, mainly in the area of the lights, which on the operational locomotive were round whereas on the model square units were portrayed. Slight revision of the buffer beam piping also prevailed with the omission of the second main reservoir pipe on the driver's assistant's side.

Author's Collection

The locomotive design office of the Director of Mechanical & Electrical Engineering (DM&EE) at Derby produced a sizeable model of the projected new standard freight locomotive during the late 1970s, which, as can be seen from this illustration is almost identical to the finished product.

Derek Porter

The main objectives of the Class 58 design were:
1. Economy in construction.
2. Ease, economy and minimum maintenance requirement.
3. Adaption to export market (to any track gauge).

The opportunity was also taken to incorporate a number of modifications that had come about following building and operational experience of the Class 56s.

It was decided that British Rail Engineering Limited (BREL) Doncaster Works would undertake the Class 58 building programme and in September 1979 work began on the manufacture of jigs and tools required for the 'new' modular construction system. The first underframe joist was cut and formed in the newly assembled jigs in Spring 1981 and the first frame was finished the following August. Problems in drilling the complete frame section, which was well over 60ft long meant that it had to be transported by road to a Sheffield steelworks. This procedure was repeated for the two subsequent frames, but thereafter all were dealt with on a new manipulator/drilling rig installed at Doncaster. Whilst this equipment was extremely costly, compared to the movement and outside industry costs of taking frames to Sheffield, the cost of installing the equipment did break even if cost was spread throughout the build. Of course, if the export market had been successful the financial benefits would have been far more significant.

The first two frames were returned to Doncaster after drilling, and entered the work's 'E2' shop, alongside the final members of the Class 56 build. Once in situ, the task of fitting out began. After return to Doncaster the third frame was mounted on a bogie bolster and taken to the Railway Technical Centre (RTC) at Derby where stress and strain tests were effected.

The initial Class 58 order was for only three locomotives, however while construction was being carried out, this was first increased by 11, and during 1982-4 subsequent orders increased the production run to 50 members.

Unlike the Class 56s, which were body assembled in the fabrication shop, only the main frames for the Class 58s were assembled in this shop, which comprised of side, end and well plate members, the frame then being transferred to the New Build (E2) shop where general assembly was carried out. The cab, cooler group, and all side components were pre-formed in the fabrication shop and transferred to the New Build shop area for installation. During the period of fitting out, the body was mounted on shop supports and a scaffold surround was erected to conform with Health and Safety requirements. The Class 58 construction programme was based on the following timescale: 12 weeks fabrication, 12 weeks main erection, 6 weeks finishing off (including painting and testing) – in all an eight month programme from plate steel to an operational locomotive. This timescale was considerably extended for the first eight locomotives in the face of supply problems, and extended time for works tooling. After completion in the New Build shop the locomotives were wheeled and transferred to the paint shop for cosmetic attention, and finally to the test house for static tests before an 'on-line' trial.

No. 58001 was completed in late 1982 and officially handed over to BR on 9th December, however considerable testing was still to be carried out and the locomotive remained under M&EE control for some weeks. After

eventually leaving the works, No. 58001 passed to the Railway Technical Centre at Derby when 'on-line' tests were carried out. By the end of 1983 seven locomotives had been handed over, all allocated to Toton depot near Nottingham.

As the Class 58s were dedicated freight sector locomotives the new *Railfreight* corporate colours were applied. Cab ends were painted in conventional yellow, extending around the length of the full width cab with black window surrounds, the back section of the cab module being painted black, as was also the top of the frame plate forming the external connection between the two cabs. The body was finished in grey with the main frame sides in red, together with the buffer beam. Under the driver's side window the running number was applied in black, the diagonally opposite corner carrying the *Railfreight* insignia in white on a red background, large BR double arrow logos being applied in the centre of the grey body panelling. Before the official handing over of No. 58001, the locomotive was painted with various livery modifications, including black buffer beams, black *Railfreight* name, and frame differences. Since construction some locomotives have been named, in most cases the *Railfreight* insignia has been removed from under the driver's assistant's side window, where the nameplates have been fitted, and replaced by a cast *Railfreight* name on the front end.

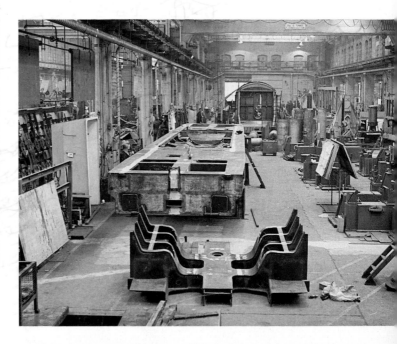

Left: The main underframe assembly was formed in the works fabrication shop, where the end, side and top members were assembled into the rigid frame. In this view of frame No. 8 (eventually locomotive No. 58008) the side joists are being offered to the end members for welding. At this point in time the frame is inverted for ease of assembly.

Colin J. Marsden

Below left: The fabrication of the frame for locomotive No. 58001 was effected in June – August 1981 alongside the final Class 56 body frames. This view taken on 21st August shows the completed frame of No. 58001, awaiting transfer to a Sheffield steelworks for drilling. In the background the shells of Class 56s Nos. 56114/115 can be seen.

Colin J. Marsden

Right: Being of modular construction, whilst the frame was being fabricated the main body components were being assembled, in various shops around the Plant. Here we see a cab assembly in its raw state prior to any fitting out. The cab sections or modules were usually completed some weeks before they were required for installation, and the actual order of construction did not reflect the locomotive onto which they were installed.

Colin J. Marsden

Below: To enable major components to be constructed with ease and efficiency special jigs were built which manipulated parts to give the most suitable working position. Here a cooler group shell is seen on a manipulator during an early stage of assembly.

Colin J. Marsden

Body

The all steel underframe is designed to carry all static loads imposed by the locomotive equipment, and those arising from dynamic forces when the locomotive is operating. In addition, the underframe is designed to withstand an end load of 200 tonnes at buffer height. Also the lifting of the complete locomotive at the centre pivots without permanent deformation of any item. The main frame is of the channel type to house both air and electrical conduit. On the original drawings this was to be left open to the elements, but on the finished product external panelling was applied. The bodysides are of a bonnet type with nine access doors to equipment compartments on either side, all of which are based on modular design for ease and economy of maintenance.

Each locomotive is formed of six modular units which are bolted to a rigid frame – each part being fully interchangeable with a stock item, enabling locomotives to be out of service for only the minimum amount of time due to any collision or major failure. The six body modules are:

Cab module x 2
Radiator module
Power unit module
Turbocharger module
Electrical module

The two cab modules are identical at both ends of the locomotive.

Between Cab Layout

The radiator module: Houses the radiator equipment and one electrically-driven traction motor blower. Radiator mountings, ducting, fan cowls and fan motor supports are incorporated.

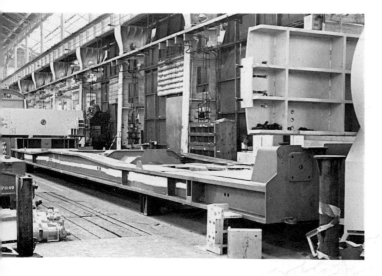

Once the underframe unit was completed in the fabrication shop, and in the case of the first three returned from drilling, the first 23 locomotives were placed in the works E2 shop and onto a manipulator which could lift and rotate the complete frame to enable top/under and side construction. Regrettably the first manipulator installed was too weak for its task and had to be replaced by a far larger unit. The frame of No. 58002 is seen in the original manipulator on 15th October 1981.

Colin J. Marsden

Power unit module: This houses the Ruston 12RK3ACT power unit, together with its alternator group. Access to each side of the power unit is by means of large bodyside doors. Compartment also contains one air compressor.

Turbocharger module: The turbocharger air inlet and electrical equipment is all housed in this small section.

Electrical (clean air) module: This section houses the main electrical control equipment, main rectifier, second electrically driven traction motor blower, and all the brake control equipment.

A continuously welded sealing plate is provided under the power unit to prevent oil spillage leaking through to the bogies. A sump with a convenient drainage point is formed in the sealing plate beneath the diesel engine. The between cab bonnet has four removable roof sections, which give complete access for the removal of equipment.

Cab Assembly

Driving cabs are provided at both ends, and are of fabricated construction, formed in steel and fully insulated against both heat and sound. Particular attention was paid to the general layout of the cab in terms of comfort and convenience for the crew. The cab layout adopted was formulated after much consultation between engineers, BR management, and the driver's trade union representatives of both ASLE&F, and NUR. The cab layout has been used as 'standard' for the next generation of diesel locomotives, and has indeed been incorporated in the General Motors Class 59 locomotives. The cab front windows are divided by a centre pillar into two large flat panes of high impact glass, incorporating built-in electric heating and defrosting. Air operated windscreen wipers are fitted at both windows, together with high-pressure windscreen washers. Adjustable front vertical sunblinds are also provided for driver comfort as are self-levelling seats. The cab side windows are of the horizontal sliding type, giving the driver or his assistant a good rearward view with the least discomfort. Robust doors give access from the cab to a transverse walkway, which has fixed glazed doors to the outside. Each cab has a single driving position arranged on the left-hand side with an assistant's position on the right. All driving instruments, switches, warning lights and controls are mounted on a conventional console-type desk. (See driving cab illustration).

The majority of driving controls are of the established type and the power controller is very similar to that incorporated in the Class 47 and 56 locomotives. The brake controllers for both locomotive and train braking are of a new (PBI) design with the established rotary moving valve giving way to a push (apply) – pull (release) handle with a central lap (hold) position. The brake controllers have no air connections at all, and are only an electric switch which sends signals to a brake control unit. A driver's emergency brake plunger is provided on the driver's desk.

Bogies

The bogies manufactured by BREL Crewe Works were of the CP3 type, similar to those experimentally fitted to Class 56 No. 56042 in May 1979 and subsequently tested. The wheels are of the monobloc type.

The main bogie frame is of welded construction, formed of two main longitudinals of box construction incorporating substantial castings connected by cross members which are a mixture of castings and fabrications. The first completed Class 58 type bogie was the subject of extensive stress and strain tests by the Research Division at Derby in early 1982. The bogie frame is supported from the axleboxes by the primary suspension consisting of helical springs in a vertical plane and silentbloc parallel rubber bushes in the lateral and longitudinal plane. The other axleboxes are each fitted with two roller bearings and the centre boxes are fitted with cylindrical roller bearings to allow lateral float. The Brush TM73-62 traction motors are axle hung, nose suspended machines. A bogie pivot pin guides bogie rotation and transmits all traction and braking forces from the bogie to the frame/body. Rubber cushions are provided in the bogie frame to give resilience to the pivot pin. Secondary suspension is by means of Flexicoils, there being three springs per side, fitted into pockets in the underframe of the locomotive.

Direct acting brakes are provided, one brake cylinder per two blocks, and two cylinders per wheel. All brake cylinders are fitted with automatic slack adjusters, taking up brake rigging as brake blocks wear. Sanding equipment is fitted which applies sand to the leading axle of each bogie in the direction of travel, control of the sanding equipment being by the driver.

With detailed plans on an adjacent easel the frame of No. 58007 is seen at a 45 deg. angle on the revised manipulator on 9th December 1982, the day the first locomotive was handed over to the operators.

Colin J. Marsden

After drilling in Sheffield the third Class 58 frame was transported to the Railway Technical Centre in Derby for strain and stress tests, the movement was on BRV bolster No. B946212, and is seen in this illustration awaiting despatch.

Derek Porter

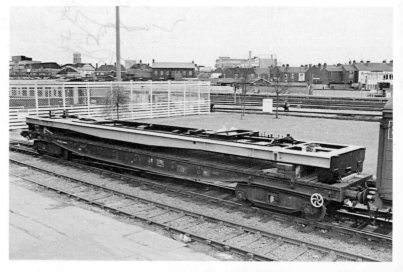

Main Power Equipment

Engine: The diesel engine, located centrally in the locomotive body, is a Ruston-Paxman RK3ACT charge air-cooled 12-cylinder engine, continuously rated at 2,610kW at 1,000rpm. It has a BMEP of 16.9 bar, although as fitted to the Class 58 locomotive it is slightly derated to 2,460kW (15.9 bar BMEP). The engine is a four stroke turbocharged type, with a cylinder bore of 10 in, and a piston stroke of 12 in. The mean piston speed is 10.2 m/s and arranged in two banks with an included angle of 45 deg. The engine is of monobloc construction and is completely enclosed. Neither the engine compartment nor radiator is accessible by the train crew, and so the Class 58s are the only BR owned main-line locomotives in traffic for which the motive power staff do not have duties to perform in the power unit compartment. Engine lubricating oil and cooling water are circulated by pumps mounted on the engine and spur gear driven from the free end of the crankshaft.

Fuel injection is by a separate fuel pump, one fitted for each cylinder. Fuel is injected mechanically into open type combustion chambers. The engine is controlled by a hydraulic servo-type variable speed governor operating the fuel pump racks. Speed control is operated by means of varied air pressure governed by the position of the locomotive's power controller and linked with an electrically operated load-control system which automatically relates the load on the alternator to the required output setting. A power take off is provided at the free end of the power unit to drive the hydrostatic pump for the radiator fan motors and their air compressors.

After return from the Sheffield steel works the frame of No. 58002 is seen resting on the floor of the works E2 'new build' shop awaiting space on works stands. Note the conduit clips were already installed.

Colin J. Marsden

Engine starting is by twin dc electric motors engaging upon a geared ring attached to the engine flywheel, and operation of the engine start button supplies power to the start relays which automatically engages each starter motor pinion in turn. (This is repeated until a successful engagement has been made.) When both motors are in mesh, relays apply the full battery power to the motors.

Cooling Equipment: The engine cooling group consists of two single bank radiator panels which cool the engine jacket coolant. The coolant is circulated through the system by engine driven pumps. Thermostatic control of fan speed is provided to permit rapid warming up of the coolant, and to maintain operating temperature. Engine air intake to the turbocharger, at the alternator end of the engine is by ducted air direct through cartridge type disposable filters located in the clean air compartment.

Alternators

Particular attention was paid to the alternators with interchangeability, and ease of maintenance. The alternator group comprises a main and auxiliary machine, each having its own brushless exciter. The main alternator rotor is built on a hollow hub which is solidly coupled to the engine crankshaft through a coupling adaptor. A solid flanged shaft extension which forms the auxiliary alternator rotor and carries both exciter rotors, is bolted to the main alternator hub and is supported at its outer end by a roller bearing. The stator assembly consists of two fabricated shells, one carrying the main, and the other the auxiliary and exciter stators. The two shells are bolted together through an end frame integral with the auxiliary shell. The stator assembly is flange-mounted to the engine. The set is self-ventilated, the fan being mounted on the coupling adaptor. Air is drawn in through the end frame and exciter shell and discharged through side openings.

The main alternator: The main alternator is a three phase, 12-pole, star connected machine. The stator core is constructed of high permeability, low-loss segmental stampings built up on dovetail keys which are bolted to pads in the stator frame. This allows cooling air to pass over

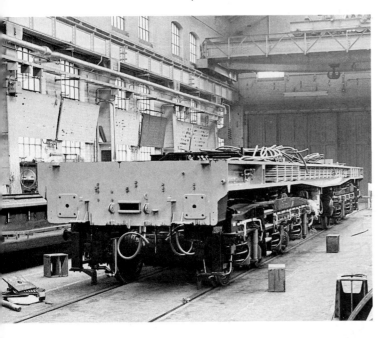

It was usual construction practise to build the complete locomotive before wheeling, however when this illustration of No. 58027 was taken on 20th November 1984 the bogies and most underframe equipment had been installed, but there was no sign of above frame construction at all.

Colin J. Marsden

the outside of the stator in addition to that through the vent holes. The stator is clamped between robust end-plates which have fingers to support the stator teeth. Diamond-type high-tension coils wound with copper, insulated with polyester enamel and silicon impregnated braided glass are used for the stator windings and are held in place by slot wedges.

The rotor hub is a one-piece alloy steel forging, bolted and dowelled to the coupling adaptor. Poles are secured to the rotor hub by high-tensile steel studs which are screwed into tapping bars in the pole laminations. Robust end-plates clamp the pole assembly. The coils are wound from braided glass insulated strip and are resin bonded to the pole bricks, adequate ground insulation being provided between the coil and pole.

The auxiliary alternator: The auxiliary alternator is a three-phase, eight-pole, star connected machine. The stator is constructed from high permeability, low-loss, one-piece stampings keyed to landings in a stator barrel which forms part of the fabricated shell containing the two exciters. The stator pack is clamped between robust end-plates, thicker stampings being fitted at the core ends to support the stator teeth. Diamond-type high-tension coils wound with copper, insulated with polyester enamel and silicone insulated braided glass, are used for the stator windings, which are held in place by slot wedges.

The rotor shaft extension is a one-piece alloy steel forging bolted to the main alternator hub. Poles are secured to the shaft with high tensile steel bolts which seat on bars in the pole laminations. As on the main alternator robust end plates clamp the pole assembly, the coils being wound from braided glass insulated copper strip and are resin bonded to the pole bricks. Again, adequate ground insulation is provided between the coil and pole.

Alternator exciters: The two exciters have their stator cores pressed into barrels in a common shell with the auxiliary alternator. The armature cores are carried on landings of individual hubs and mounted on to a common sleeve which also carries the dual rotating rectifier assembly. The sleeve is fitted onto a tapered seating on the shaft extension. The stator and rotor laminations are formed into packs and retained by welding and riveting.

Traction Equipment

Traction motors: The Class 58 has six traction motors, supplied by Brush Electrical Machines (BEM) and designated TM 73-62. They are a direct derivative of those used on the Class 47 locomotives, the high-powered 'prototype' HS4000 *Kestrel* built by Hawker Siddeley and, in more recent years the Class 56. Attention was paid to robustness combined with light weight, interchangeability, ease of maintenance and life expectancy.

Each traction motor has four main poles, four compoles, four brush arms and is designed for axle mounting and nose suspension. The motor is force ventilated by a duct system, air being provided by two body mounted motor blowers via flexible ducting at the commutator end of the frame. The air is then passed through ventilation ducts provided in the armature core, and along the outside of the armature and through the space between field coils. It is finally ejected at the pinion end.

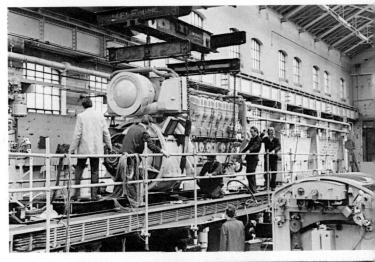

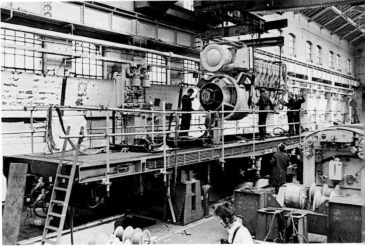

The Ruston Paxman 12RK3ACT power units were constructed at the Ruston Works in Newton le Willows and transported to Doncaster by road for the delicate job of installation onto the frame. With side scaffolds to prevent men falling from the frame, No. 58001 receives its power unit in this 14th April 1982 illustration, under the watchful eye of some of the senior production staff.

Both: Derek Porter

Some time after the power unit and other ancillary equipment had been fitted, including the traction motor blower visible in this illustration, the main cooler group was installed, which itself was an independent module.

Derek Porter

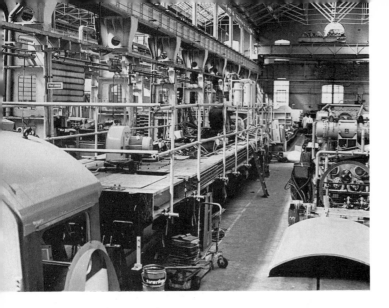

The provision of a scaffold surround on the frame during fitting out was a Health and Safety requirement, as it would have been quite easy for a man to slip from the side. Hitherto when in the course of constructing locomotives, the body sides have offered protection. The frame of No. 58002 is seen taking shape on 31st August 1982.
Colin J. Marsden

During July 1982 the cab modules were fitted and for the first time the appearance of the locomotive started to become apparent. In this view the completed cab is seen being lowered by overhead crane into its fixing locations. The fitter second from right is commencing the securing procedure, whilst others guide the cab into its resting position.

Colin J. Marsden

Axle Suspension: Traction motor axle suspension is by means of a Timken suspension tube fitted with a taper roller bearing at each end. Grease lubrication is employed.

Gear drive: The motor pinion drives a solid spur gearwheel mounted upon the axle. The gearwheel is machined from a steel forging with its teeth induction hardened. The pinion, manufactured from an alloy steel forging, has a taper ground bore and is shrunk on to a similarly tapered armature. The pinion being case-hardened after cutting and the teeth are subsequently ground to remove any distortion caused by heat treatment. In addition, the pinion teeth are relieved towards the motor side by grinding, to avoid undesirable load concentration. The gears are enclosed in a robust case which is made in two parts, the joint between these parts being shrouded to prevent the entry of any dirt or moisture or the escape of the lubricant. The case is bolted together at the ends and is supported on the motor by three brackets, one above and one below the axle, the third being at the pinion end.

Traction Control

Power circuits: The six traction motors are arranged in three series pairs, except under slow speed control. Each pair is switched by an electro-pneumatic contactor. In the event of traction motor problems, pre-selected pairs (one traction motor from each bogie) can be isolated by means of a switch housed in the electrical compartment at No 2 end. One stage field diversion is provided. A single three-circuit electro-pneumatic reverser controls the direction of current flow through the motor fields, thus controlling the direction of the locomotive. A high speed short-circuiter operated under fault conditions is connected across the output terminals of the rectifier, to divert fault current away from the traction motors and prevent any damage. The field winding is supplied from the electronic load-regulator. Overcurrent relays are fitted around each of the alternator output cables, and are designed to operate should a main rectifier diode fail. The driver's cab ampmeters are supplied from a ring-type current transformer around one of the alternator cables.

Rectifier unit: There are six vertically disposed aluminium heat sinks, each carrying four silicon diodes connected in parallel. Across each set of four diodes is connected a storage capacitor. The heat sinks are cooled by an air flow drawn through the rectifier from top to bottom by the alternator.

Slow speed control system (SSC): As the Class 58 locomotives were intended for merry go round (MGR) coal and possibly other mechanised load traffic, a slow speed control (SSC) system was incorporated, which is selected by a switch in the cab. The six traction motors are then connected in series. The engine speed under SSC is set at a constant 450 rpm. The driver can select one of four pre-set speed settings (0.5 mph, 1.0 mph, 2.7 mph, balance). The balance speed will provide a 'balancing speed' according to the load of the train against the traction power available with the engine at idling rpm. On an average gradient the position will produce a speed of 7-8 mph to assist in moving away a heavy train when rail conditions are poor. Under the SSC mode the speed is sensed by two traction motors. The train speed is then automatically controlled, the driver simply controlling the brake as necessary.

Wheelslip correction system: Electronic wheelslip detection is necessary due to the high tractive effort capability of the locomotives and the arduous duties encountered when hauling heavy trains under poor rail conditions, which are frequently met on power station and colliery lines. The wheelslip detection system operates on the principle of comparing traction motor currents. When a wheelslip is detected the traction alternator excitation volts are rapidly removed, thus cutting the tractive effort. When wheelslip has stopped the tractive effort is restored to a level slightly lower than that pre-set before wheelslip, the reduction being proportional to the time wheelslip occurred. Thus severe or repeated wheelslip reduces the subsequent tractive effort substantially, in turn reducing the tendency to cause further slipping.

Traction motor faults: In the event of a traction motor blower or a pair of traction motors being isolated, the engine speed, and hence the output, is automatically restricted so that damage will not occur to equipment still in operation.

Braking system: The Class 58 fleet is only fitted with air brake equipment, a straight air brake for the locomotive, and a train air brake system giving a proportional application on the locomotive. A modified E70 brake control system has been adopted for use on the fleet, since it offers several advantages over conventional brake systems using pneumatic driver's brake controllers, such as simple cab/cubicle layout, and the omission of large diameter air pipes in the driving cab. The system also offers the potential for fully automatic operation in the future if required, this system being based on the equipment tested on Class 56 locomotives Nos 56073/74 in the late 1970s. The driver controls the auto brake by means of an electrical brake control switch which energises a combination of three wires in a sequence corresponding to pre-determined brake values. The brake pipe pressure control unit converts the controller brake demand on one running and seven brake applications into auto air brake pipe pressure. The standard Automatic Warning System (AWS) and the modern vigilance device, where the driver has to release the driver's

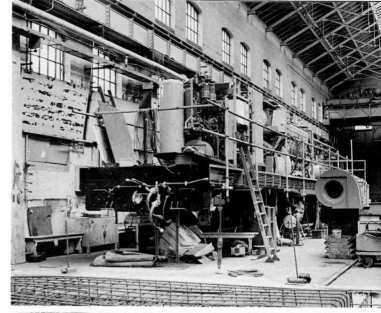

Top: For a number of reasons, not the least being a locomotive of a totally new design, No. 58001 was assembled without any of its modular section covers until nearing completion. On 16th May 1982 the locomotive is seen in the E2 shop with some 80% of its internal fittings already installed.

Colin J. Marsden

Above: It was usual practise that once the frame was complete and the underframe equipment installed, the cab sections, which had been previously assembled in another shop, were fitted. No. 58008 is seen in E2 shop on 5th July 1983, some four weeks after entering the shop from the fabrication area.

Colin J. Marsden

After the first locomotive was completed a number of minor livery variations appeared, one of the most noticeable to staff at Doncaster was that when constructed, Nos 58001-03 had black buffer beams, whereas all subsequent machines were constructed with the beams in green primer, for eventual painting in red. No. 58003 is seen under construction in the 'new build' shop in December 1982.

Colin J. Marsden

safety device pedal each time an alarm sounds (every 60 secs) is fitted as standard. The locomotives are also equipped for Driver Only Operation (DOO), being fitted with a Slow Speed Fitting (SSF) unit whereby the brakes are automatically applied to a full emergency pressure if the driver neutralises the master switch when the locomotive is travelling at a speed above 9 mph.

A hydraulically applied and released parking brake is fitted, the required pressure being generated by an electrically driven pump. The parking brake operates on only two wheels of one bogie, and is applied by using the parking brake push buttons in either driving cab, or by emergency controls located in the transverse walkway at No 2 end.

Locomotive Operation

The design of the Class 58s is such that up to three locomotives may be operated in multiple. At the present stage it is not envisaged that train consists requiring three Class 58 locomotives will be introduced, but the feature has been incorporated to allow operating flexibility in the future. The same multiple control system, conforming to the red diamond type, is fitted to the Class 56 fleet so inter-coupling is possible.

Sepex

Following the introduction of the General Motors Class 59 locomotives owned by Foster Yeoman in 1986, BR were very impressed by the traction characteristics and creep control system incorporated, enabling extremely heavy train consists to be moved in adverse rail conditions. When the final Class 58 was under construction it was announced that a 'Sepex' control system was to be installed in an attempt to improve the locomotive's traction characteristics and wheelslip problems. The equipment developed by Brush was installed at BREL Doncaster in late 1986 and consisted of a pick up under the driver's side buffer which 'read' rail conditions and gave signals to the locomotive's traction control equipment. Although the equipment was similar to that installed on the Class 59s, many problems were encountered with the equipment, resulting in the locomotive not entering revenue earning traffic until August 1987. Initial reports have indicated that the modifications have increased the hauling power of the locomotive.

The projected timescale for a Class 58 to be under construction in the 'new build' shop was twelve weeks, however due to late deliveries of many components from outside manufacturers, as well as delays with 'on works' production, this period was often extended. No. 58005 illustrated here was admitted to E2 shop on 23rd December 1982, but was not sent to the paint shop until August 1983, a timescale well outside the requirement.
Colin J. Marsden

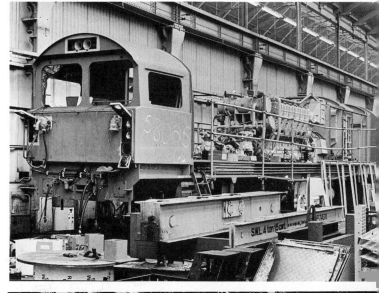

Right, above: After some 23 locomotives had been built, due to a reorganisation within the works the remaining 27 examples were constructed in the main 'Crimpsall' area. No. 58025 in a 50% complete condition is seen in 2-Bay on 20th November 1984.
Colin J. Marsden

Right: From the often apparent cluttered atmosphere it was a minor wonder that any Class 58s ever emerged from Doncaster! On 3rd May 1986 No. 58043 is seen supported on works accommodation stands in 2-Bay, only some four weeks prior to completion.
Colin J. Marsden

Above: The first time a Class 58 was seen outside the erecting shop was on 17th September 1982, when No. 58001 was hauled by Class 08 No. 08776 from the 'new build' E2 shop to the flash test booth in the paint shop. The locomotive is seen emerging from E2 shop in this illustration.

Derek Porter

Above, right: After its completion No. 58001 was the subject of much technical and cosmetic attention within the confines of the works. During November when the locomotive was almost resident in the test house a number of different 'Railfreight' logos were applied to gauge the best eye-catching effect. This photograph shows a black 'cut-out' Railfreight logo.

Colin J. Marsden

Right: Nearly the end of the line, No. 58048 is seen, inside the works 4-Bay on 4th October 1986, with the locomotive's No. 1 end being nearest the camera. The cab in the foreground was labelled for the penultimate locomotive No. 58049, but was in a far from complete condition.

Colin J. Marsden

Below: Only the first locomotive emerged from the new build shop in a painted condition, the balance were dispatched from their birth place in green works primer. No. 58004 is seen in the paint shop yard on 7th August awaiting admittance for cosmetic completion.

Peter Gater

The official handing over day of the first Class 58 was 9th December 1982, when a press launch was arranged, and the locomotive ceremoniously driven through a red plastic screen in front of the works offices. This illustration shows the locomotive bursting through the screen watched by Mr.E. Marshall, one of the senior works staff involved in the production of the fleet.

Colin J. Marsden

Although the locomotive was handed over to the operating department in December 1982 it did not venture onto the main line until Spring 1983, and then only at the head of test and training specials. No. 58001 is seen approaching Doncaster station at the head on a Doncaster – Immingham special.

Derek Porter

After the Class 58s were completed in the new build shop, and cosmetic attention had been given, the test house took over, to thoroughly evaluate all electrical, and mechanical components before the locomotive was permitted to travel on the main line. On 20th November 1984 No. 58020 *Doncaster Works BRE* is seen inside the test house, while main alternator monitoring was being carried out.

Colin J. Marsden

Technical Description

Class	58
Number Range	58001 – 58050
Built By	BREL Doncaster
Introduced	1983-87
Wheel Arrangement	Co-Co
Weight (operational)	130 tonnes
Height	12 ft 10 in (3.9 m)
Width	8 ft 10½ in (2.70 m)
Length	62 ft 9½ in (19.13 m)
Min Curve negotiable	4 chains (80.46 m)
Maximum Speed	80 mph (129 km/h)
Wheelbase	48 ft 9 in (14.85 m)
Bogie Wheel Base	13 ft 8½ in (4.18 m)
Bogie Pivot Centres	35 ft 5½ in (10.80 m)
Wheel Diameter (driving)	3 ft 8 in (1.12 m)
Brake Type	Air
Sanding Equipment	Pneumatic
Heating Type	Not fitted
Route Availability	7
Multiple Coupling Restriction	Red Diamond
Brake Force	62 tonnes
Engine Type	Ruston-Paxman 12RK3ACT
Engine Horsepower	3,300 hp (12,460 kW)
Power at Rail	2,387 hp (1,780 kW)
Tractive Effort	61,800 lb (275 kN)
Cylinder Bore	10 in (0.25 m)
Cylinder Stroke	12 in (0.30 m)
Main Alternator Type	Brush BA1101B
Aux. Alternator Type	Brush BAA602B
Number of Traction Motors	6
Traction Motor Type	Brush TM73-62
Gear Ratio	63:16
Fuel Tank Capacity	985 gal (4,480 lit)
Cooling Water Capacity	264 gal (1,200 lit)
Lub Oil Capacity	110 gal (416 lit)
Allocation	Toton depot, LMR
Sector Ownership	Railfreight – Coal

With Washwood Heath Yard as a backdrop. No. 58013 heads towards Water Orton on 5th February 1985 with a rake of 24 empty HBA type 'Railfreight' coal hoppers.

Colin J. Marsden

Cab Layout

Class 58 cab layout. It was decided at the same time as the design work was underway for the Class 58, to introduce a standard diesel locomotive cab layout and this was fitted on the Class 58s, and from staff reaction proved very popular. When the privately owned Class 59s were introduced for British operation the same cab layout was used with minor detail differences involving the power control pedestal.

1- Automatic air brake controller (train/loco.), 2- Direct brake controller (loco. only), 3- Horn switch (high/low note), 4- Emergency brake plunger, 5- Parking brake 'on' push button, 6- Parking brake indicator, 7- Parking brake 'off' button, 8- Brake overcharge release button, 9- Main reservoir & main reservoir pipe pressure gauge, 10- Brake cylinder pressure gauge, 11- Brake test indicator light, 12- AWS in/out indicator light, 13- Engine stopped indicator light, 14- Brake pipe & control reservoir pressure gauge, 15- AWS alarm, 16- AWS 'sunflower' indicator, 17 Wheel slip indicator, 18- General fault indicator, 19- Speedometer, 20- Slow speed control speed selector switch, 21- Driver's side screen wash/wipe switch, 22- Slow speed control speedometer, 23- Main alternator ampmeter, 24- Engine start button, 25- Engine stop button, 26- Fire alarm test button, 27- Crew communication buzzer button, 28- Crew communication buzzer, 29- Fire push-button, 30- Hotplate control switch, 31- Driver's assistant's side screen wash/wipe switch. 32- Heat/ventilation control switch (fan), 33- Heat/ventilation control temperature, 34- Power controller, 35- Master switch (Off/Rev/Eo/For), 36- Driver's key socket, 37- AWS reset button, 38- Cab-cab telephone. The cab illustrated is from No. 58017.

Colin J. Marsden

Fleet List

Number	Name	Date Named	Date Introduced
58001	–	–	May 1983
58002	–	–	May 1983
58003	–	–	July 1983
58004	–	–	September 1983
58005	–	–	October 1983
58006	–	–	October 1983
58007	–	–	November 1983
58008	–	–	December 1983
58009	–	–	January 1984
58010	–	–	February 1984
58011	–	–	March 1984
58012	–	–	March 1984
58013	–	–	March 1984
58014	–	–	April 1984
58015	–	–	September 1984
58016	–	–	October 1984
58017	–	–	October 1984
58018	–	–	October 1984
58019	–	–	November 1984
58020	Doncaster Works BRE*	November 1984	November 1984
58021	–	–	December 1984
58022	–	–	December 1984
58023	–	–	December 1984
58024	–	–	January 1985
58025	–	–	January 1985
58026	–	–	March 1985
58027	–	–	March 1985
58028	–	–	March 1985
58029	–	–	March 1985
58030	–	–	June 1985
58031	–	–	September 1985
58032	–	–	September 1985
58033	–	–	September 1985
58034	Bassetlaw	December 1985	November 1985
58035	–	–	January 1986
58036	–	–	February 1986
58037	–	–	February 1986
58038	–	–	February 1986
58039	Rugeley Power Station	September 1986	March 1986
58040	Cottam Power Station	September 1986	March 1986
58041	Ratcliffe Power Station	September 1986	March 1986
58042	Ironbridge Power Station	September 1986	May 1986
58043	–	–	July 1986
58044	–	–	August 1986
58045	–	–	September 1986
58046	–	–	October 1986
58047	–	–	October 1986
58048	–	–	December 1986
58049	Littleton Colliery	March 1987	December 1986
58050	Toton Traction Depot	May 1987	March 1987

*When No. 58020 was named the plate read *Doncaster Works BRE,* but this was not favoured by the Company management and during 1987 the plates were replaced by new ones carrying just the name *Doncaster Works.*

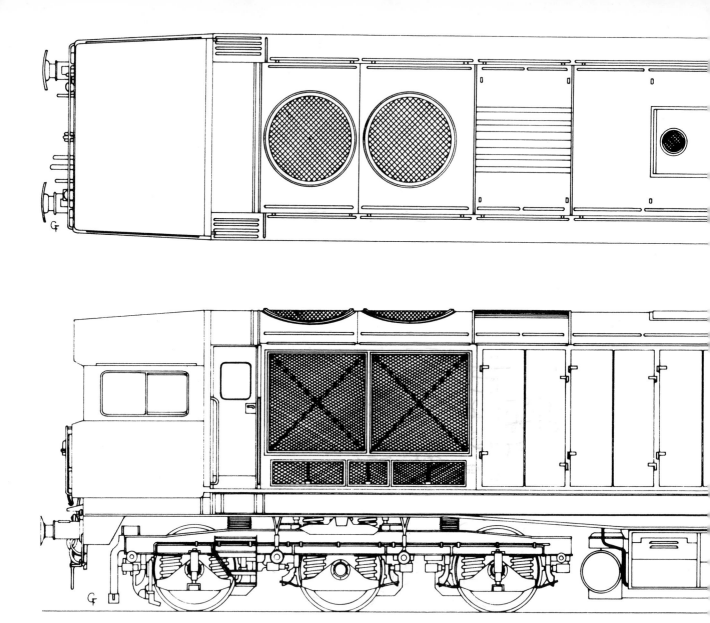

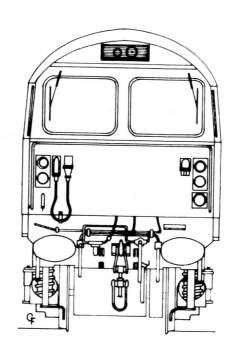

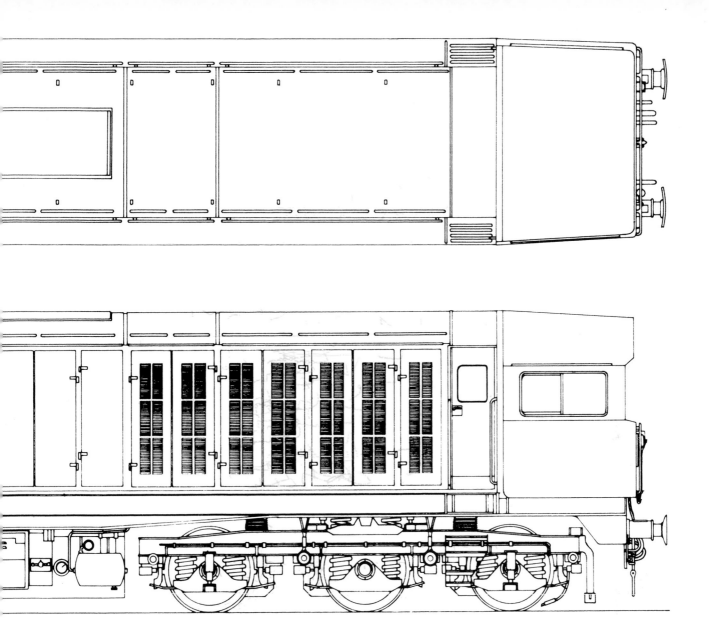

Top: Class 58 roof layout, locomotive No. 1 end being on left.

Above: Class 58 side elevation, with the No. 1 end on left. This drawing applies to locomotives Nos 58001-14 only, after which engine room door handles were fitted. The cab sides also received ventilation grilles from locomotives No. 58036.

Left: Class 58 front end layout, applicable to all locomotives of the build.

Scale 6 mm = 1 ft

All drawings have been kindly supplied by Mr. G. Fenn.

Performance

by M.J. Oakley

At the time of writing, it is possible to hear the Class 58 being described as the first specialist freight-only locomotive built for British Rail, which it is not. Its physical appearance provokes violent disagreements, and its relatively limited sphere of operations makes it an unknown quantity to many enthusiasts. In particular, the few passenger workings on record have mostly been railtours over slow-speed coal lines, so that little flat-out performance data is on record. The 58, then, is a locomotive sadly lacking in definition for most people.

To understand the Class 58 in performance terms it is necessary to place it in historical context. The history of diesel development in Britain is littered with the casualties of two conflicting trends – on the one hand the desire to standardise mechanical equipment for simplicity and economy of scale, and on the other, the need to adapt to changing traffic patterns. It is ironic that coal, which gave many railways their impetus in the first place and which has changed little in its pattern of operation since, should be one of the key factors which forced mechanical change, and continues to do so.

Thus the declining and fragmenting general freight traffic in the early years of BR dieselisation was not surprisingly reflected in a mixed policy and mixed results in freight locomotive design. Most small, early types were harder-worked on passenger duties, simply because such work exposed more immediately their limitations. Lack of power resulted in low-geared designs simply because there was no choice, and the slow pace of freight movement did not require anything better. This in turn allowed the concept to grow up of diesel power being capable of all-embracing "mixed-traffic" design.

The initially 2,750 bhp Brush/Sulzer Class 47 was the ultimate such design – one which can be called successful in that it did the jobs it was set within its limitations in the first instance. It was no fault of the locomotive design that sweeping changes in traffic patterns undermined its position; rather it was an unfortunate combination of accidents. In order to accommodate the available power of the locomotive to a wide speed range, it had to be 'geared between two stools'. As an express passenger type it was stretched to the odd maximum of 95 mph, but at a cost of substantial "unloading" above 82 mph. As a freight type it was not to be trusted at low speed for any length of time, giving it a hopelessly high continuous rating speed of 27 mph.

One particularly unfortunate combination was enough to finish the mixed-traffic locomotive as far as BR were concerned, and that was the Clarborough Effect. Widespread introduction of merry-go-round working with modern hopper wagons for coal traffic had made greatly increased loadings possible, where the route would permit. On level track, roller-bearing axleboxes and high vehicle capacities both contributed to a substantial reduction in rolling resistance, and it is well within the capacity of even a Class 47 to work four-figure tonnages at 60 mph running

There have been relatively few occasions that the locomotive performance buffs have had a chance to calculate the performance of the Class 58s, except on a few railtours and substitutions for booked motive power. On 28th July 1984 the RESL's "The Plant Invader" railtour was operated from Waterloo to Doncaster, motive power being provided by No. 58010 which is seen leaving Sheffield on the return working.

John Tuffs

During the construction of the Class 58s a number of projected performance figures were supplied by both BREL, and the equipment manufacturers. However after the first locomotive was in traffic BR's own performance tests were carried out using Derby based test car No. 6, which is seen here coupled to No. 58001 at Leicester Junction near Burton-on-Trent on 31st August 1983.

John Tuffs

Traversing the usual stamping ground of the Erewash Valley, No. 58010 is seen again at the head of the "Plant Invader" railtour of 28th July 1984 near Westhouses. This railtour took participants to Doncaster Works to enable them to inspect the Class 58 production line on the occasion of the works Open Day.

Peter Gater

speeds. Not so on the uphills, where work required increases inexorably with total train weight. The flow of coal from the Sheffield area towards the South East has a mostly level run via the Lincoln route to March, but at Clarborough Junction near Retford it encounters an upgrade of 1 in 120 with a 20 mph speed restriction due to subsidence. Sustaining this speed, or more often 10-15 mph, up the bank with a full load proved sufficient to undo the 47s, with repeated instances of overheating damage to the traction motors.

The answer eventually found was the Class 56, in which design policy went back with a bang to the traditional idea of a separate freight design. Just what freight was intended does not seem to have been clear, at least at the top end of the performance range, as a curious maximum speed of 80 mph was fixed while no freight goes faster than 75. However, in practise the 56 became almost entirely a creature of the coalfields, so attention was rightly centred on its performance at the lowest speeds. Part of the solution was to install greater engine power, so as to get up the gradients that much faster where needed, or drag ever-increasing tonnages where that was preferred. More important still, the critical continuous rating speed was arranged to be 16 mph, giving much increased scope for all-out slogging. The Class 56 story came to be overshadowed by the curious decision to build the first thirty in Roumania, and the consequent shortcomings of a variety of minor matters; but of one thing there has been no doubt,

and that is the ability of the locomotives to actually get their trains up the hill as required.

Although differing in numerous other respects, the performance of the Class 58 is essentially identical to that of the 56 in the first instance. Where the two types have worked alongside each other, they have been treated as interchangeable, the only differences in work being that the 58s have been restricted to fewer routes for non-performance reasons. The 58 has also become almost entirely a creature of the coalfields, working mostly on short distance hauls from collieries to the nearest power stations. The longest regular working of note has been from Toton to Didcot, but the bulk of the coal is burned by the string of power stations along the River Trent. The Trent-coalfield area happens to have a high proportion of routes from which passenger trains have been withdrawn, notably the Mansfield/Shirebrook group, so little is seen of them in the normal way.

The now terminus of Matlock provided the 'end of the line' for the F&W Railtours 'The Coalville Slug' tour from Penzance on 1st September 1985, which was hauled by No. 58018 and is illustrated at Matlock.

Peter Gater

The first time a Class 58 hauled a passenger train out of King's Cross was on 20th September 1986 when No. 58039 *Rugeley Power Station* hauled the ''Lincolnshire Coast Pullman'' railtour from King's Cross to Skegness and Cleethorpes. The train formed of the 'Pullman Rail' stock is seen approaching Doncaster.

Les Nixon

The few examples which have ventured onto passenger trains have comprised a few summer Saturday emergencies on the Lickey route, and a few special enthusiast railtours. Matters have been severely limited by only a few depots having trained their crews on the class, resulting in such oddities as all the first five known passenger workings going past Trent power signalbox, in every possible combination of directions! With the much lighter weight of passenger trains – at 80 mph on the level a train of twelve MkII coaches has a rolling resistance of only 1,025 horsepower – flat-out performance opportunities are limited on their own account as well. A few bits of inviting upgrade occur on main lines, best of all the 1 in 100 climbs between Chesterfield, Sheffield, and in the Hope Valley; otherwise the recorder has to make the best of the rapid accelerations from stops where the gradients happen to be constant, such as the first couple of miles out of Leicester where the gradient is actually falling slightly.

The accompanying logs show about the best that can be done in the circumstances. Horsepowers calculated across violent accelerations, and/or of only a couple of minutes' duration, are probably accurate only to within plus or minus about 5% at the best of times. Those involving steady speeds on 1 in 100 upgrades are more reliable but do not show what variation in output there may be relative to speed. It is unfortunate that little or no data ever gets recorded or published about coal train work at lower speed. From what results can be obtained, however, it is apparent that very little variation in output against speed does occur once under way. In particular the 80 mph limit is very much a law of man rather than of nature, as one or two of the more fun-loving drivers have shown. With the amount of power available, it has been shown that a 56 or 58 can be pushed well past the limit and into the nineties, there being very little effect to compare with the amount of electrical unloading featured in earlier designs.

One further point which can be made is that laws of statistics apply to horsepower calculation, just as to anything else. Providing the selection of data is random – which in these illustrations it certainly is, there being effectively no choice – averaging out a number of performances at similar speed should produce figures with proportionately reduced margin for error. Then it is possible to make a more reliable comparison between designed and actual performance. The actual performances calculated at thirteen points in the five recordings referred to, average out to an equivalent drawbar hp of 2,615 at 61.3 mph. In the absence of any data for locomotive wind resistance, a conservative estimate of 175 hp at this speed gives a rail hp of 2,790. This is derived from known data for earlier BR types, the likelihood being that the "hood" bodyside of the 58 is more streamlined, but that this will be more than outweighed by that hideous slab front end. Lastly, reference to the only known tractive effort curve for Class 56/58 (such things being a notorious source of imprecision) suggests that 2,790 bhp corresponds to a crankshaft horsepower of 3,630. Within the likely margin for error, 3,630 is near enough to the 3,520 bhp officially quoted for the class at the time of its design. An efficiency of 86% from crankshaft to drawbar is certainly feasible in a modern locomotive of such power, and is a rather more likely figure for properly maintained locomotives than the 79% which would obtain 3,520 bhp rather than 3,250. Nevertheless 3,250 is now the official figure. The continuous rating value is 2,387 hp at the rail, but a maximum a few hundred higher than this is likely higher up the speed range. Class 58 performance therefore sits in the unresolved limbo of performances which just don't add up, for the moment at any rate.

For the future it is another aspect of performance entirely which continues to exercise the engineers: that of adhesion. In steam days there was simply no alternative to relying on the skill of the driver to find the best adhesion level possible. Adhesion increases with speed, so steam express locomotives with large wheels could easily go into a spin on starting, before settling into speed. Diesel designs likewise started off by leaving things partly to the driver. Diesel-hydraulics in particular can be arranged to accept full engine power from a standing start, in which circumstances tractive effort (power divided by speed) is theoretically infinite. Within the normal demands of passenger working such fine points were largely academic, trains normally getting into speed too quickly for it to make much difference. Some limitation was applied to the maximum tractive effort obtainable in practise, and several classes had the figure reduced after service experience. Few drivers start off using anything like the power theoretically available anyway, it is simply unnecessary to do so.

Very different criteria apply with today's heaviest freight trains, which are the MGR-style stone workings out of the Mendip quarries and up the awkwardly-graded Berks & Hants line towards London. The possibility of stalling on the climb to Savernake with several thousand tons of stone makes tractive effort a much more important consideration than horsepower – once again modern vehicles with low rolling resistance make hauling the load at full speed the easy part of the job. Acquisition by quarry owners Foster Yeoman of their own American-built Class 59 locomotives, for which superior starting characteristics are claimed, has been the spur to further experimentation by BR engineers with a view to doing the same. Although the Sepex-fitted final Class 58 is slated for experimental use to this end, the likely outcome is a further new design, Class 60 with a maximum speed of 60 mph only for the heaviest freight work alone.

Historical context therefore places the Class 58 firmly as an intermediate design in the progress from mixed-traffic to even-more-specialist freight-only locomotion. As a structural and financial improvement on Class 56 it was undoubtedly a justified development, but as a performance duplicate it represents a consolidation of existing standards, a drawing of breath. Some of its capabilities are certainly breathtaking by comparison with what went before. Ironically it is going down not as one of the most-noticed locomotives in proportion, but as one of the least.

Sunday 18th September 1983.
58 Pioneer railtour.
Locomotive: 58002.
Load: 11 vehicles MkI/II stock, 374/400 tons.

m c			m s	speeds
0-00	NUNEATON		0.00	–
4-16	Hinckley		5.58	67/66
7-25	Elmesthorpe		8.37	73/67
12-02	Narborough		12.37	68/sigs 24
15-42	Wigston N.Jn.box		16.56	30/64
18-57	LEICESTER	=21¼	22.21	–
0-34	Milepost 99½		1.25	29½
2-34	Milepost 101½		3.36	72/77
4-58	Syston		5.23	76/78
9-66	Barrow-on-Soar		9.23	77/sigs 42
12-41	Loughborough		12.15	55
15-26	Hathern		14.42	78
20-76	Trent box		19.23	64*
22-70	Attenborough		20.59	78
27-41	NOTTINGHAM	=26	27.09	–
3-25	Beeston		5.41	66/74
6-45	Trent box		9.16	14*
9-68	Draycott		15.04	69/sigs
15-76	DERBY	=22½	25.24	–
3-19	Little Eaton Jn.		4.40	75/77
7-63	Belper		8.14	75
10-30	AMBERGATE		12.45	–
3-06	High Peak Jn.		5.15	49/52
6-62	MATLOCK		10.40	–
3-56	High Peak Jn.		5.04	53
6-62	Ambergate		9.35	–
2-47	Belper		5.00	68
7-11	Little Eaton Jn.		8.30	80
10-30	DERBY		12.12	–
3-64	Borrowash		5.15	76/pws 46
9-19	Trent Jn.		10.38	63*
16-70	Loughborough		16.46	78/76
24-53	Syston		22.52	78
29-31	LEICESTER	=27¾	28.30	–
3-15	Wigston N. Jn. box		5.43	56/pws 22
6-55	Narborough		11.05	58/72
11-32	Elmesthorpe		15.14	67½
13-61	Milepost 4¾		17.15	72½
14-41	Hinckley		17.52	74/sigs
18-57	NUNEATON	=22¼	24.43	–

Calculated power output:-
1 in 500 fall MP 99½ – MP 101½: 2,625 edhp at 55.0 mph.
Level Loughborough – Hathern: 2,370 edhp at 68.9 mph.
1 in 162 rise Elmesthorpe – MP 4¾: 2,570 edhp at 70.3 mph.
*Speed restrictions

Sunday 15th July 1984.
South Yorkshireman railtour.
Locomotive: 58014.
Load: 10 Vehicles MkII stock, 326/350 tons.

m c			m s	speeds
0-00	BIRMINGHAM New St.		0.00	–
3-20	Washwood Heath Jn.		5.33	62/sigs 10
7-50	Water Orton		12.19	29*/49
10-32	Whitacre Jn.		16.48	pws 20/48
16-56	Arley Tunnel W. end		29.42	pws 28/69
20-77	NUNEATON	=24	37.10	
4-16	Hinckley		6.59	sigs/71
7-25	Elmesthorpe		9.17	77/81
12-02	Narborough		12.59	69/75
15-42	Wigston N. Jn. box		16.30	38*/sigs
18-57	LEICESTER	=20½	30.48	–
0-34	Milepost 99½		1.20	32
2-34	Milepost 101½		3.30	73
7-42	Sileby		7.24	78
12-41	Loughborough		11.07	83
20-76	Trent box		18.15	32*/45
22-62	TOTON centre box		21.34	–
4-64	Ilkeston Jn.		6.23	pws/77/pws 20
8-05	Langley Mill		11.04	61*
14-19	Alfreton & M.P.		16.34	75/80
20-31	Clay Cross		21.34	64*/78
24-32	CHESTERFIELD	=22¾	26.28	–
2-00	Milepost 148½		5.08	sigs/56
5-00	Milepost 151¼		8.03	64
6-29	Bradway Tunnel S. end		9.17	66½ att/69
8-00	Dore		10.59	44*/78/sigs
12-21	SHEFFIELD	=15	20.43	–
0-40	Pond St. Tunnel S. end		1.46	33
2-41	Milepost 156		4.21	56 att
4-21	Dore		7.02	sigs 14
6-77	Dronfield		11.32	67/88
12-21	Chesterfield		19.24	sigs 0/70/35
16-22	Clay Cross		23.50	50
22-38	Wingfield		28.56	83
26-39	Ambergate S. Jn.		32.11	55*
31-11	Duffield		35.42	90/92
36-32	DERBY	=32¼	43.48	–
4-54	Stenson Jn.		5.02	87
8-68	Clay Mills Jn. box		7.38	96½
11-01	Burton-on-Trent		9.14	57*
16-44	Wichnor Jn.		13.34	90/92½
19-54	Elford		15.45	pws 18
23-72	Tamworth		23.20	52
29-36	Kingsbury		27.40	92/95½
33-47	Water Orton		30.28	73*/83
37-77	Washwood Heath Jn.		34.29	pws/sigs 18
41-17	BIRMINGHAM New St.	=33¼	41.53	–

Calculated power output:-
1 in 500 fall MP 99½ – MP 101½: 2,480 edhp at 55.4 mph.
1 in 100 rise MP 148¼ – MP 151¼: 2,655 edhp at 61.6 mph.
1 in 100 rise Pond St. – MP 156: 2,575 edhp at 46.7 mph.
*Speed restrictions.

Sunday 12th August 1984.
Paxman Collier railtour.
Locomotive: 58013 outward, 58006 return.
Load: 12 vehicles MkII stock, 391/425 tons.

m c			m s	speeds
0-00	BIRMINGHAM New St.		0.00	–
3-20	Washwood Heath Jn.		5.53	65/70
7-50	Water Orton		11.27	pws/23*/59
10-32	Whitacre Jn.		15.20	27*/52
16-56	Arley Tunnel W. end		26.31	pws 22/67
20-17	Abbey Jn. box		31.20	28*/18*
25-05	Hinckley		38.14	66
28-14	Elmesthorpe		40.54	72
32-71	Narborough		45.00	67/72
36-31	Wigston N. Jn. box		48.55	32*/63
39-46	LEICESTER	=48	54.24	–

m c		m s	speeds
0-34	Milepost 99$\frac{1}{2}$	1.56	32
2-34	Milepost 101$\frac{1}{2}$	4.04	73
4-58	Syston	5.48	82
9-66	Barrow-on-Soar	9.58	pws 47
12-41	Loughborough	12.57	72/80
20-76	Trent box	19.33	sigs 0/54
27-41	NOTTINGHAM	= 26	38.05	

m c		m s	speeds
0-00	TOTON Stapleford	0.00	–
2-47	Trent box	5.24	48/sigs/12*
6-66	Castle Donington	13.55	44/pws 21
11-30	Chellaston Jn.	21.35	39/47
15-51	Stenson Jn.	28.32	19*
16-16	North Staffs Jn.	29.24	50
19-55	Clay Mills Jn. box	32.26	80
21-68	Burton-on-Trent	34.21	53*/80
25-54	Barton	37.55	pws 20/78
30-41	Elford	44.20	pws 18
34-59	Tamworth	49.35	78/80
40-23	Kingsbury	53.48	76/82
44-34	Water Orton	57.01	70*/80
48-64	Washwood Heath Jn.	61.14	pws/sigs 10
52-04	BIRMINGHAM New St.	= 58$\frac{3}{4}$	68.12	–

Calculated power output:-
1 in 500 fall MP 99$\frac{1}{2}$ – MP 101$\frac{1}{2}$: 2,925 edhp at 56.3 mph.
Average level North Staffs Jn. – Clay Mills Jn.: 2,535 edhp at 69.0 mph.
*Speed restrictions

Saturday 8th September 1984.
13.40 Poole to Sheffield.
Locomotive: 58007.
Load: 10 vehicles MkII stock, 333/350 decreasing 345 tons.

m c		m s	speeds
0-00	BIRMINGHAM New St.	0.00	–
3-20	Washwood Heath Jn.	4.39	63/70
7-50	Water Orton	9.40	pws/27*/63
10-32	Whitacre Jn.	13.15	31*/59
16-56	Arley Tunnel W. end	22.45	pws 31/69
20-77	NUNEATON	= 22	29.17	–

4-16	Hinckley	5.14	74/80
7-25	Elmesthorpe	7.40	78/pws 35
12-02	Narborough	12.13	47/67
15-42	Wigston N. Jn. box	17.01	sigs stop
		20.32	–
18-57	LEICESTER	= 20$\frac{1}{2}$	26.55	63 max

0-34	Milepost 99$\frac{1}{2}$	1.02	43
2-34	Milepost 101$\frac{1}{2}$	2.57	76
7-42	Sileby	6.52	78/79
12-41	LOUGHBOROUGH	12.03	–

0-13	Milepost 111$\frac{3}{4}$	0.37	29
2-65	Hathern	3.19	77/79
8-35	Trent box	7.58	67*/77
10-29	Attenborough	10.04	pws 17
10-73	Milepost 122$\frac{1}{2}$	11.21	39
12-33	Milepost 124	12.57	69
15-00	NOTTINGHAM	= 15	17.03	–

(Locomotive worked through Birmingham to Sheffield)

Calculated power output:-
1 in 500 fall MP 99$\frac{1}{2}$ – MP 101$\frac{1}{2}$: 2,580 edhp at 62.5 mph.
Level MP 111$\frac{3}{4}$ – Hathern: 2,675 edhp at 58.9 mph.
Level MP 122$\frac{1}{2}$ – MP 124: 2,800 edhp at 56.3 mph.
*Speed restrictions

Sunday 16th September 1984.
Midland Macedoine railtour.
Locomotive: 58007.
Load: 10 vehicles MkII stock, 333/360 tons.

m c		m s	speeds
00-0	DERBY	0.00	–
3-64	Borrowash	5.12	80
9-32	Trent box	13.02	sigs 1/72
13-24	Stanton Gate	16.54	69*/80
16-02	Ilkeston Jn.	19.04	75*/pws 15
19-23	Langley Mill	23.38	63/75
21-75	Codnor Park	25.54	62*
25-37	Alfreton & M.P.	29.01	78/75
28-65	139m 35c summit	31.40	77/75
31-49	Clay Cross	34.02	sigs 55/79
35-50	Chesterfield	37.24	sigs 32
37-50	Milepost 148$\frac{1}{4}$	39.39	68
40-50	Milepost 151$\frac{1}{4}$	42.17	68 sus/69
41-79	Bradway Tunnel S. end	43.28	67*
43-24	Dore S. Jn.	46.02	13*
48-18	Grindleford	52.23	68/58*
51-72	Bamford	55.49	73/63*
54-50	Earles Sidings box	58.18	67
58-44	Edale	61.48	67$\frac{1}{2}$ sus
59-66	Cowburn Tunnel E. end	62.55	68/72
63-32	Chinley S. Jn.	68.38	sigs stops
		77.53	
67-47	Peak Forest	85.11	42/pws 5/42
70-29	Peak Forest Jn.	92.29	16*/41
74-18	BUXTON Jn. box	= 82	99.03	

0-00	BUXTON	0.00	–
2-18	Dove Holes summit	4.38	47 att/59
5-23	Chapel-en-le-Frith	8.40	35*/56
9-06	Whaley Bridge	13.11	54/sigs 0
11-40	New Mills	18.30	46/sigs 15/59
16-68	Hazel Grove	24.56	50/54/sigs 0
19-74	Stockport	34.57	16*/60
22-74	Levenshulme	39.25	sigs 28/53
25-63	MANCHESTER Piccadilly	= 34$\frac{3}{4}$	44.53	–

2-69	Levenshulme	4.07	69/74/sigs 0
5-69	Stockport	12.42	19*/sigs 15
8-16	Cheadle Hulme	17.50	38*
13-23	Adlington	22.43	79
17-69	Macclesfield	27.47	sigs 23/0
22-33	North Rode Jn.	38.50	66/79
25-56	Congleton	41.24	76*/80
31-24	Kidsgrove	45.45	74/76/pws 46
34-62	Longport	49.08	72/74
37-55	STOKE-ON-TRENT	= 38$\frac{1}{4}$	53.07	–

2-29	Longton	5.21	47/pws 25
5-62	Blythe Bridge	10.20	69/sigs 35
10-66	Leigh	15.30	69/70
16-68	Uttoxeter	22.04	25*/68
21-24	Sudbury	27.12	sigs 49
27-39	Egginton Jn.	32.41	69
30-48	North Staffs Jn.	35.46	37*/71
34-45	Pear Tree	40.11	pws 47/49
35-76	DERBY	= 40	43.54	–

Calculated power output:-
1 in 100 rise MP 148$\frac{1}{4}$ – MP 151$\frac{1}{4}$: 2,615 at 68 mph sustained.
1 in 100 rise past Edale: 2,590 edhp at 67$\frac{1}{2}$ mph sustained.
* speed restrictions

(m c = miles and chains: m s = minutes and seconds).

Above: The more usual consist for a Class 58 is a rake of MGR hopper wagons, which provide some 95% of the fleet's diagrammed work, and it is virtually impossible for the performance enthusiasts to travel on such trains, unless they sit with the coal! On 10th April 1986 No. 58019 approaches CEGB West Burton Power Station with a loaded 34 vehicle train.

Les Nixon

Below: One of the most interesting Class 58 diagrams, at least to the photographers was the Toton – Arpley, and Ashburys – Toton ABS freight which operated in 1984-85, as the train often conveyed only one or two vehicles. However, the train was far from economic and it ceased to operate from Summer 1985. On 16th February 1985, when the train was well loaded No. 58010 passes Edale with the Toton bound service.

Les Nixon

Class 58 Tractive Effort Curve

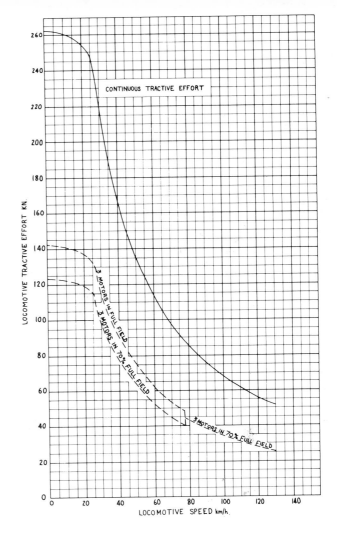

No. 58022 pulls away from Tolworth on 23rd October 1987 with an empty rake of HBA 'Speedlink' coal hopper wagons, forming the daily Chessington – Didcot working.

Colin J. Marsden

Locomotive Maintenance

by Simon Hartshorne of The Class 58 Locomotive Group

All British Rail Locomotives undergo regular preventative maintenance and Class 58's are no exception. The reason is simple, mechanical and electrical components suffer wear and tear and without this maintenance the reliability of any machine would be in doubt.

Since a locomotive is essentially several hundred components and machines bolted together, the recipe for failure is clear to see. In order that these failures are kept to an absolute minimum (and the customer is kept happy) each locomotive undergoes detailed and regular inspections at pre-determined intervals. Some of the components, by the very nature of their design and use, are more reliable than others, a Main Alternator for example which runs at more or less constant speed and load is far less prone to failure than the brake rigging which is constantly subjected to differing stresses and temperatures. This is borne in mind when the maintenance schedules are being drawn up.

There are six categories of examination and between them they ensure that all necessary items on the locomotive are examined and checked for defects and correct operation over a period covering approximately $4^1/2$–5 years (the period between classified intermediate overhauls).

Because of the type of work on which Class 58's are used, scheduled examination takes place as far as possible at weekends in order that the maximum number of locomotives are available for hauling trains during the week. (Current usage demands that 80% of the fleet, ie 40 locomotives, is available each day).

The owning depot is alerted of forthcoming examinations by means of the TOPS (Total Operations Processing System) computer. Operators enter details of all train, and thus locomotive, movements into the system so that a picture emerges of the number of TOPS hours run up by each locomotive. When built the locomotives are on zero TOPS hours, as they are used and run up the hours the computer will "call" a locomotive slightly before it becomes due for scheduled maintenance. At the beginning of each week a list is printed out for the Maintenance Controller at the owning depot – Toton in this case – telling him which locomotives are due (and in exceptional cases overdue) for maintenance and what type of examination is due.

The only depot ever to have had an allocation of Class 58s is Toton, near Nottingham from where the locomotives are deployed by the Railfreight's coal sector on the numerous MGR duties that emulate from the nearby area. Class 58 No. 58050 named *Toton Traction Depot* during 1987, is seen outside the north end of the shed in this May 1987 illustration.

Colin J. Marsden

Examination Schedules

As the locomotives run in service the engineers who look after them gain experience and are aware of the components which are liable to need more attention than others. With this in mind they, in consultation with the staff at Toton, are able to draw up accurate maintenance sheets which dictate what component is examined and when. Quite often in the light of experience they are able to increase the amount of time between examinations because the components are found to be more reliable than previously thought.

As mentioned earlier there are six categories of examination, which are as follows:

Fuelling Point (or Service Check) exam.

A exam	–	every 80 hours
B exam	–	every 400 hours
C exam	–	every 1,200 hours
D exam	–	every 3,600 hours
F1 exam F2 exam	–	every 7,200 hours*

*Considered as one exam – see text for details.

It would be possible to fill a whole book with examination details alone so it is the intention here to only cover the main points of each examination, and in the process it is hoped to reveal some of the maintenance mysteries that exist in engineering circles.

The two major workhorses allocated to Toton depot are Classes 56 and 58, both of which are illustrated outside the south end of the depot. The Class 58 can clearly be identified as No. 58043, while the Class 56 is No. 56025, one of the Roumanian built examples.

Colin J. Marsden

A **Fuelling Point** exam (sometimes known as a Service Check) is, as its title suggests, carried out every time the locomotive is fuelled. Although this period can vary from once a day to once every five or six days, depending on the diagrams, it is always at the same intervals as far as usage is concerned. It is not a detailed examination and only takes about 15 minutes. When the locomotive arrives on the fuelling point it is met by a fitter who will first attach fuel and coolant hoses and fill the respective systems to capacity. He will then check the Driver's Repair Book (in the cab) for any defects reported by the operating staff during the course of the day's workings.

Any defects found are dealt with in one of two ways; serious defects such as a brake problem or a suspected electrical earth fault will require the locomotive to be moved to the maintenance shed for fault finding/rectification immediately. The locomotive will then be deemed "out of service" until such time as the defect is found and corrected and the locomotive has been tested. The locomotive will not be taken back into service, before the Driver's Repair Book has been endorsed with the relevant details of any fault found and the action taken being signed off by the fitter/electrician concerned and the shift supervisor. If however the reported fault cannot be detected then the book is endorsed "NDF" (No defect found) and signed off by the fitter/electrician.

Contrary to popular opinion BR takes a dim view of service failures and should a locomotive disgrace itself whilst in traffic, many enquiries are made to determine the case of the failure and the names of those involved with its last exam or repair.

Less serious defects however such as a driver's assistant's side windscreen wiper not working or minor leaks, ie faults which do not affect the immediate reliability of the locomotive, are normally left until the next exam (if one is imminent) or at least until the weekend when valuable service times would not be lost.

During the cab visit the fitter will keep an 'eye' open for any item which although not of a serious nature may cause consternation amongst train crews and therefore prevent the locomotive from being taken into service. This being things such as cab lights not working, damaged seats and faulty or broken switches. Also items in contradiction of the Health and Safety act, rags or waste paper likely to cause fire, loose or damaged footsteps likely to cause accident or injury.

Once outside the locomotive the fitter checks the brake blocks for acceptable wear (minimum thickness 1 in), the brake rigging for obvious defects and then has a general walk round the locomotive looking for loose or otherwise defective covers, panels, air hoses and drawgear. Finally the windscreen, marker and tail lights, headlights and the high visibility panels are cleaned and the sandboxes filled. The locomotive is then assumed to be fit for service until its next exam, whether it is another fuel point check or a major overhaul.

In the laid down maintenance schedules there is a proviso stating that at each fuel point exam certain items outside the engine room must be checked, viz engine lubricating oil level and the level of oil in the radiator hydrostatic system (where applicable). However the Health and Safety regulations contradict this instruction because maintenance staff are not permitted on the side walkway without safety barriers. This in practise means that these

Under the 1987 revision of BR's locomotive maintenance policy, Toton became a level 4 depot, which entitles it to carry out all required maintenance and overhauls except component exchange for which Doncaster level 5 depot has to be used. This view shows the two lifting roads on the west side of the depot occupied by Class 58 No. 58028, and Class 56 No. 56083.

Colin J. Marsden

It is usual to find some 2% (four locomotives) receiving classified attention at TO at any one time, however this can be drastically increased at weekends when very few machines are at work. Standing adjacent to the 'platform' height walkways Class 58s Nos. 58011 (left), 58002 (right) share depot space with a Class 56 and Class 20. Note the deep illuminated inspection pits.

Colin J. Marsden

To provide easy access for internal inspections all the side doors and most of the roof sections can be removed. No. 58017 is illustrated with its engine compartment open in this May 1987 view. On the right a pair of 'Railfreight' Class 37/5s are seen.
Colin J. Marsden

items go unchecked between main exams when the locomotive is usually inside a shed, but this has not been found to be detrimental to the locomotive's reliability however as these systems currently suffer minimal leakage, unlike the same systems on some older classes of locomotive.

A Exam
The first level of classified exam is an "A Exam", carried out every 80 hours. Following a visit to the fuel point (locomotives are normally fuelled on arrival at a depot, as a precautionary measure to prevent the embarrassing problem of running out of fuel should they be called into service suddenly). At Toton depot the locomotive would be run onto one of the platform roads where the entire exam will be carried out. An A exam is mainly a series of functional tests where items are physically checked for operation and rectified when found to be defective. In addition, components will be changed or repaired if it is thought that they might cause failure before the next scheduled exam.

The following items are examined for damage from outside the locomotive and with the engine shut down, unless special circumstances dictate otherwise; the AWS receiver and associated cabling and hanging brackets, the brake blocks, the brake rigging, the buffers, the bodyside and underframe, the bogies, battery boxes and air reservoirs, the wheels and tyres and the fixed BCF (Bromochlorodi-flouromethane) locomotive fire extinguishers.

Back inside the locomotive, before carrying out the tests which require the engine to be running, the oil levels in the engine sump, hydrostatic system (where applicable), compressor sumps and engine governor are checked and topped up as necessary. All the remaining checks demand that the engine is running; when it is and with all the bodyside panels and doors removed (allowing superb access to the engine and its auxiliaries) checks are made on the general engine sound and condition, it is checked for clear exhaust (ie not black or smoky), unusual noises, leaks of fuel, oil or coolant, even running, and that each cylinder is firing (checked by overfuelling each cylinder in turn and listening for the relevant bang!).

Whilst in the engine compartment about half a pint of the coolant and lubricating oil is drawn off from cocks for chemical analysis. This plays a very important part in the effective maintenance of all diesels as it is possible to predict premature engine failure by spectrographic analysis of the lubricating oil. For example a high proportion of aluminium indicates piston trouble, whereas fuel in the lubricating oil suggests a leak around the high pressure pipes in proximity to the cylinder heads. In these and all others cases the lubricating oil would be changed immediately and remedial action taken to prevent further deterioration of engine condition. Even during the short life of the Class 58 many engines have already been 'saved' from major failure because of spectrography. The coolant is similarly checked for foreign bodies and also for additive strength. Class 58 coolant is treated with a chemical known as Borax Sodium Metasilicate – essentially used to keep the coolant pipes clean and free from corrosive substances.

In the cab now and to the functional part of the exam, all of the following items are checked in both cabs as obviously each cab employs separate control systems. In the cross corridor at the number 2 end is the hydraulic parking brake control unit – its oil level is checked on the way to the cab.

The operation of the straight air brake (for controlling the locomotive brakes only and sometimes known as the direct air brake) is checked and any defects being noted and repaired.

One of the many safety systems fitted to all British Rail locomotives is a Driver's Safety Device (DSD). This takes the form of a pedal fitted immediately in front of the driver and must be kept depressed at all times while either forward or reverse direction is selected. If the pedal is released for more than six seconds the Brake Pipe Pressure Control Unit will destroy the brake pipe air and the brakes will be applied at full pressure. A hold-over button is fitted at the driver's assistant's side so that the driver may leave his seat (for the purpose of shunting etc) and use this button to prevent any brake application. The operation of the DSD is checked from both these positions. A vigilance device is also fitted to these locomotives through the DSD pedal and is checked for operation. Finally, before leaving the cab, the sanding gear is operated and checked for free flowing and good delivery to the running rails. In addition to the above, the items cleaned at a fuelling point exam are cleaned again, viz windscreen, lights, high visibility panels etc.

B Exam
The first of the "major" exams takes place every 400 hours which equates to approximately 6–8 weeks depending on diagrams. Each B exam lasts about eight hours and again would be arranged for weekends wherever possible. All the exams above an A exam are a repeat of almost all the work done on the previous exam and include extra work necessary to check various other items. The following extra jobs are carried out at a B exam. Inside the engine room the lubricating oil level of the radiator fan drive gearbox (where fitted) is checked and the numerous bodyside air filters changed. Air management is one of the design points of the Class 58 and so it is important that the correct airflow is achieved.

Internal cleanliness is important as mentioned earlier and with this in mind the cabs, cross corridors and auxiliary compartments are cleaned therefore minimising the risk of fire and accident. From beneath the locomotive, all components mentioned in respect of the A exam are checked as well as visually inspecting all six traction motors for internal damage, such as flashovers or fires. While the covers are removed from the motors the length and condition of the brushes are checked and any which are, or will be before the next exam, below 1 in or are damaged, are changed. Traction motor brushes are a vital part of reliable locomotive operation and their importance cannot be overlooked. While under the locomotive a check is made on the bogies and they are greased at the numerous points provided, likewise the buffer shanks and faces and the draw hooks and coupling screws.

Batteries are provided primarily for engine starting and a poorly charged or otherwise defective set of batteries would cause a locomotive failure and as a locomotive failed is not a locomotive earning money, a close check is kept on battery condition. In particular the maintenance staff are looking for broken or damaged connecting straps and dry cells. Cells may dry out for many reasons, a cracked and leaking cell case, or overcharging of the battery by the auxiliary voltage regulator being the most common causes. Usually if one cell is not holding its charge it will very rapidly drain the other cells leading to a failure.

A number of spare fuses are kept on board for staff to replace any which may rupture whilst the locomotive is away from the depot. The quantity and rating of these fuses is checked in the No. 2 end cross corridor.

Back in the cab, and with the locomotive in a serviceable condition (ie engine running and air reservoirs charged) the automatic air brake operation is checked using master gauges attached to the buffer beam hoses as well as the normal cab mounted gauges. This has the advantage of confirming the accuracy of the cab gauges as well. The method of automatic air brake application and release is almost unique at the moment and is only used on Classes 58

and 59. Since electrical pulses are used to control brake pipe pressure via a control unit a far more accurate and infinitely variable pressure range is available for braking, and because it employs fewer mechanical valves than a conventional locomotive it is far more reliable. Many tests are incorporated into the automatic air brake test, but the main objective is to ascertain the time taken to apply the brake, the time taken to release the brake and the control unit's ability to hold correctly the brake pipe pressure over a period of some ten minutes.

Fitted to the switch panel above the driver's seat is a brake control switch. It has two positions, 'Service' and 'Isolate', and is used when a brake test is being carried out by a guard or shunter. During a brake test it is necessary that the brake pipe is completely isolated from the main reservoir and brake valves and the switch performs this function. Following a successful brake test the switch is returned to the 'Service' position and allows the brake pipe to be recharged and the brakes released. The operation of this switch is checked during the examination.

A functional AWS test, ie checking for correct operation, is carried out by simulating the AWS track magnets using a hand held testing magnet on the receiver beneath the locomotive and noting the sequence of events in the cab.

C Exam

A "C exam" takes place at 1,200 hours, which is about every 26 weeks. Such is the time spent out of service at this exam (some 16 hours plus any additional time for extra work) that provision is made for it in the locomotive diagrams. As will be seen it involves checks on many of the larger machines as well as the components previously mentioned under A and B examinations.

Taking the exam in the same order as before, in the engine compartment, the compressor drive shaft bearing is greased – this is a shaft which takes power from the free end of the engine and turns a flywheel driving the two air compressors on either side of the locomotive. Air for the compressors must be clean and to ensure this it is drawn through oil-wetted air filters mounted in the bodyside doors adjacent to the compressors; these filters are now changed. The engine lubricating oil system uses a replaceable element filter to keep the engine free of small particles dangerous to the engine and this is changed as are the similarly responsible fuel filter elements. Before the fuel reaches the felt filters from the pump it passes through a small gauze metal strainer which removes any larger contaminants, the strainer is examined for damage and cleaned in diesel oil.

As the exhaust is open to the atmosphere, it is susceptible to rainwater, some of which will inevitably find its way through the silencer and into the turbocharger. The presence of water in such a highly stressed piece of equipment is not desirable, so a small bore hole is drilled at the lowest point of the turbocharger, exhaust side casing and pipework carries any water away and drains it to the outside of the locomotive. This hole and the associated pipework is cleaned to ensure good drainage.

When air is compressed (for brakes etc) it heats up dramatically and is then cooled before being fed into the main reservoir. A by-product of this process is water, which if allowed to enter the air system, could cause seizure of, and in winter, freezing of the brake system. In order to

Stabled just inside the depot building, at the north end is No. 58018, which is viewed from its No. 2 or electrical end. At weekends upwards of 30 Class 58s can be found at Toton depot – however before any enthusiasts visit the depot full written permission must be obtained from the Depot Engineer.
Colin J. Marsden

prevent the build up of water the main reservoirs are fitted with automatic drain valves which remove water by using a small reduction in air pressure such as occurs during a brake application. These are tested by slightly reducing main reservoir pressure and checking for water discharge at each drain valve.

One Man Operation is fitted to the locomotives, which is effectively an electronic device known as a speed switch. If the reverser is moved to 'Engine Only' when the locomotive is moving at more than 9 mph the brakes are immediately applied at the emergency rate and a 90 second delay is imposed before the brakes can be released. This is tested functionally by moving the locomotive under its own power, selecting 'Engine Only' and seeing if the brakes are applied.

Two more items of safety equipment to be checked are the equipment governor which prevents the driver taking power until sufficient air exists to stop the locomotive, and the low main reservoir governor which, in the event of main reservoir pressure falling below 4.3 bar, will apply the full brakes. Functional tests are made on the hydraulic parking brake, the locomotive lighting system and the cab to cab communications. The main reservoir pipe and brake pipe hoses including the isolating cocks and coupling heads are examined for damage and correct operation and changed if necessary. While at the locomotive front the draw gear is examined for damage and is lubricated.

Underneath the locomotive from a centre pit the six traction motors receive detailed attention. In addition to the visual examination previously mentioned under a "B exam", the armature bearings are greased, the gearcase securing bolts are checked for tightness as are the suspension bolts and caps. Finally the level of gearcase lubricant and the condition of gearcase seals are checked. Still outside, the

condition of the tyres and wheels are examined and the amount of wear on the tyre profile checked. The wheelsets can be re-turned on the underground wheel lathe to restore tyre profile, but are changed if they have sustained damage that cannot be turned out.

Back inside the locomotive and the auxiliary compartment comes under scrutiny. Apart from a tidiness exam already mentioned, electrical components are checked, viz traction motor contactors – these close to complete the circuit from the main alternator to the traction motors and carry some very high currents and consequently can become pitted and burnt. Such trouble is not uncommon and can lead to earth and power problems. In order to prevent this they are kept clean by removing all smoky and metallic deposits, and the actual contact tips are usually changed to preserve a smooth mating face which is conducive to reliable operation. As it would be dangerous to open the door covering the traction motor contactors with currents as high as 3.5kA present, an interlock switch is provided so that the traction motor contactors open and therefore lose all current should the door be opened. Before leaving the auxiliary compartment maintenance staff will check that all the notices warning of the presence of high current electricity are legible and replace any which are not.

Finally, in the driving cab a check is made on the driver's emergency equipment, ie the detonators, to check all are present and not out of date, the red flag is checked for damage and colour fade and the track circuit operating clips are examined for damage.

D Exam

The "D exam" is carried out at 3,600 hours, approximately equal to once every 72 weeks. This is a major exam and is again catered for in the locomotive diagrams. In common with the other exams the D exam contains all the jobs mentioned prior plus those jobs described in the paragraphs below.

The lubrication of the compressor drive shaft bearings has already been covered, taking this one step further the D exam includes a check on the condition and tightness of the Layrub Coupling bolts. A Layrub Coupling is a flexible coupling in the drive between the engine and the auxiliaries. The drive shaft splines also require lubrication. As well as a Layrub Coupling and spline drive for the compressors there is one for the cooler group (where applicable) which need the same attention.

The cooling systems work under pressure from engine driven pumps, and in order that the cooling is effective a certain pressure must be maintained and this is measured during the exam.

Exhaust fumes are poisonous and are unwelcome in the wrong places. They can also cause problems as they are extremely hot and have been known in the past to cause fires. Bearing this in mind it is important that the engine exhaust and silencer systems are complete and totally free from leaks. An examination is made on the system at regular intervals and at a D exam the silencer is removed and temporary exhaust 'stacks' fitted to enable a detailed check to take place, with the engine running and each cylinder in turn over fuelled as mentioned before. Any cracks of a minor nature are welded, more major cracks necessitate an exhaust manifold change.

Each cylinder on the 12RKCT in common with all other British Rail diesel locomotives, has its own high pressure fuel injector pump and fuel injector. Connected to each

Sharing depot space with various Class 56, 45 and 37 locomotives Class 58 No. 58012 stands at the north end of the depot on 25th February 1984. At the time this illustration was taken this locomotive had just arrived from BREL Doncaster and still awaited depot commissioning.

David Nicholas

injector pump is a control rod which in turn is connected to a fuel control rack under the influence of the engine governor. Both the fuel racks (one per bank of cylinders) and their associated connections are thoroughly cleaned of all fuel and oil deposits, checked for correct operation and then lubricated with clean engine oil, to ensure trouble free working until the next exam. The fuel injectors must operate perfectly for the cylinders to fire when required. A leaking or dribbling injector will not allow the cylinder to fire and will eventually lead to engine failure caused by excessive crankshaft strain. In order to avoid this all twelve injectors are changed and overhauled. Each cylinder also has exclusive valve gear and this is inspected for damage and the tappet clearance checked and adjusted as necessary.

As mentioned elsewhere, two different types of radiator fan operation are found on the Class 58 fleet – hydrostatic and mechanical drive. These checks are only applicable to locomotives with mechanical drive and they are the lubrication and examination of the actual fans, clutch lubrication, fan drive shaft lubrication and gearbox bearing lubrication.

Moving away from the engine compartment and on to three functional tests within the locomotive compressed air system. It must be appreciated that any system which contains gas under pressure is potentially explosive and the air reservoirs of a Class 58 are no exception. Any reservoir suspected or found to be defective at a depot is changed and sent back to the National Supply Centre for overhaul. There is a permanent safety device fitted into the system – a safety valve which is set to open and release main reservoir air pressure at 11 bar. This is checked by isolating the compressor unloader valves and observing the point at which the safety valve opens. A defective or suspect valve would be removed and replaced. Adjustments are not permitted unless set up under controlled circumstances.

If a break should occur in the main reservoir pipe anywhere throughout the train, the effect would be that all the main reservoir air would rapidly leak out of the locomotive with the predictable effects on brake efficiency. In order to combat this a Duplex Valve is fitted between the main air reservoirs and the main reservoir pipe (leading to the train). This will prevent air flowing quickly either way through it. It is tested by opening a main reservoir pipe cock on the buffer beam and noting the amount of air allowed to leak out. While at the buffer beam the pressure of the main reservoir pipe is measured and corrected if necessary (correct pressure being 7 bar).

Under the locomotive, working from within a pit the traction motor suspension bearings are lubricated, and the bellows which duct air from the traction motor blowers to the six motors are examined for defects and repaired or changed as required. Still outside the locomotive, while the batteries are on an equalising charge, all the connections are greased and the battery box is cleaned out and repainted.

Certain auxiliary switches and contactors are examined which includes checking for burning and pitting of contact tips and correct operation of relays and auxiliary contacts.

The time spent out of service for the examination allows time for the bogies and underbody to be thoroughly cleaned and degreased. This is done to minimise the risk of a fire caused by stray sparks from the brake blocks during heavy braking.

Various other work is included in the examination of a 'secondary nature' such as, door lock and hinge lubrication,

roof hatch and grille examination, cab fresh air intake filter change and cab sliding window check. A functional test of the fire bottle operating system (although without letting off the extinguishers) concludes the D exam.

F Exam

In common with other classes the Class 58 locomotives will in future be dealt with under the Component Exchange Maintenance System which replaces the Main Works Repair portion of the traditional system and complements the preventative maintenance schedule already described. When the schedules and work content of the examinations were being drawn up, the engineers were aware that when the CEM exam became due at 7,200 hours many components would not even be approaching their half life. Decisions were then made on which auxiliary equipment and engine components would be changed at the CEM examination eg. brake cylinders and engine cylinder leads and turbochargers.

It became clear that it would not be economic to change items inside the power unit, for example the camshaft and main bearings at 7,200 hours, but that they would need attention at 14,400 hours – such is the reason for two CEM exams. Expressed quite simply an F1 exam involves the changing of some of the locomotive auxiliary equipment, some remedial power unit work and regular maintenance items. An F2 involves a similar amount of locomotive work and a much more detailed power unit overhaul when a spare unit would be fitted to the locomotive to reduce its time out of service.

At the time of writing no Class 58 has undergone either F exam. Although two locomotives, Nos 58001/02 are due to be called at the beginning of the 1988 Financial year, slightly ahead of their due date, these two will be very much an investigation exercise and all subsequent F exam content will be based on information gained from the condition of these two locomotives. For example on many older classes of locomotive, a bogie overhaul would be required at this stage. Whilst the bogies will be removed and given a detailed examination on the first two locomotives, it is anticipated that minimal attention will in fact be necessary on subsequent locomotives and it may well prove more efficient to separate bogie changes from the 'F' exam as described above and treat them as an individual component exchange at the established optimum frequency.

Modifications

When any new design of locomotive is built, especially a completely new concept like the Class 58, it is inevitable that certain things will not work as planned. In the main, however, the locomotive has been a success. The commissioning team at Toton and the Railway Technical Centre, Derby have investigated failures and defects and a lot of improvements have been introduced.

The locomotives were built in two lots, lot No. 1511 (Nos. 58001–58035) and lot No. 1513 (Nos. 58036–58050), and a number of design differences are apparent between the two batches. It is difficult to deal with them in any specific order, as each in its own right is as important as the next, and each depends in most respects upon the next in order to increase reliability and availability. They do, however, fall into two distinct areas: engine and power/bogie.

Engine

The single turbo-charger as fitted to the Class relied on air pressure produced by the impeller blades to form a labyrinth seal to prevent oil flowing into the exhaust. This proved to be unsatisfactory, especially during idling conditions when the turbo-charger was not running at anything near boost pressure. The solution was to take the air supply from an external source, ie the locomotive compressed air system. This has solved the problem completely.

British Rail has a policy of dual sourcing major components on an experimental basis; one area subject to this policy is the exhaust silencer. The requirement for noise emission laid down by the European Economic Community (EEC) is to be no greater than 95 dBA at 7.5 metres from the locomotive and 1.5 metres above rail level. British Rail aimed to meet this requirement from the outset. It became obvious though, that neither of the originally fitted silencers were in line with the regulations. A modified unit of twice the original volume (1.4m³ instead of 0.7m³) was built into locomotive No. 58027 onwards and this has achieved 85 dBA at full load on static tests, but this has resulted in a total level of 96 dBA when measured as the EEC directive states. The additional noise is predominantly due to radiator fan noise at full engine revs.

Unfortunately, in the first years in traffic the engines were not renowned for their easy starting. This is one of the problems with high performance engines which rely on the turbo-charger to produce the performance and efficiency. Generally speaking, manufacturers reduce the cylinder compression ratio on turbo-charged engines to keep the cylinder pressures within reasonable limits. A consequence of this is that the heat input is too low on compression to allow the fuel to ignite. The problem is particularly bad on a cold day and this leads to the locomotives being idled more than they should. Engineers from the engine manufacturers, Ruston Paxman, were aware of this problem and they have changed the pistons and altered the spill timing of the fuel injectors. This has dramatically improved engine starting on the Class 58 with a consequent rise in availability, especially during winter.

In line with the policy of dual sourcing, the cooling system was supplied by Cov-Rad (Nos. 58005 – 58014) and Serck-Behr (Nos. 58001 – 58004, 58015 – 58035 excepting 58031). Both operate on a similar principle with minor differences. The problem is similar though. The hydraulically operated fans tend to hunt and suffer from thermic cycling which results in inefficient engine cooling. The solution was to adopt the system in use on Classes 20, 31, 37 and 40, ie mechanically driven cooling fans. However, these too have problems in that they over cool during winter. The modification prototyped on No. 58031 (and fitted as built to Nos. 58036 – 58050) was a fan drive shaft, driven from the engines free end and connected to the fans via clutches. These clutches are capable of disconnecting the fans from the drive when cooling is not demanded.

Bogies

As built Nos. 58001 – 58035 had CP3 bogies, a development of the CP1 tried experimentally under No. 56042. It is a superb unit which is capable of transmitting power well and giving excellent riding characteristics. Nos. 58036 – 58050 ride on modified bogies however. They are classified CP3a and differ from the standard CP3s in that:

i.   They have modified sandboxes allowing easier filling and incorporating a perspex cover showing the level of the contents.
ii. They supply sand to the inner wheels in addition to the outer ones.
iii. They use SAB brake units which are lighter and more compact than the Westinghouse units.

The two bogies are completely interchangeable although mixing them under one locomotive is not permitted.

Traction

The traction motors are connected in three series/parallel pairs for normal working. A permanent field divert was originally connected across one motor in each pair. This was

Although allocated to Nottinghamshire and Yorkshire coal duties the Class 58s are seldom seen at Tinsley depot. However on 7th June 1983, whilst still under test No. 58001 was photographed outside Tinsley depot adjacent to the fuelling equipment. Note the wiring looms attached to the bogies and cab of the locomotive.
Les Nixon

to counteract weight transfer, causing wheelslip at the start and was the same divert applied to all six motors above a speed of 49 mph. Originally wheelslip detection was by a current balance relay but this was not effective in detecting multiple axle clips, and the first two locomotives caused many rail burns. The system was changed to a voltage balance system which was much more sensitive and proved effective in detecting multiple axle slips and preventing rail burns. The permanent field divert was removed at the same time.

Toton TMD

Toton depot comes under the control of the Area Maintenance Engineer (Freight) and is responsible for maintenance of the entire Class 58 fleet as well as Class 56s, Class 20s, Class 08s and visiting Class 47s, Class 45s, Class 37s and Class 31s.

Approximately 450 staff are employed on maintenance duties. It is classified a Level 4 depot, under the Component Exchange Maintenance (CEM) policy. This means that if needed the depot could carry out almost all the required maintenance on the Class in theory, and so they need to visit their allocated major works for classified overhaul at Doncaster on few occasions.

There are 15 roads in the shed which comprises four through and eleven dead end roads, the latter having the platforms necessary for Class 58 and Class 20 maintenance along half their length. All tracks are equipped with deep centre illuminated inspection pits. Some dead end roads have side pits as well. These are especially useful for access to axleboxes and bogie running gear. All dead end roads have the provision to lift out equipment via overhead cranes of one ton capacity. Nos. 13, 14 and 15 roads are specially equipped with a four ton overhead travelling crane, while the latter two roads have concrete reinforced sides to enable a locomotive to be lifted for the purpose of bogie changing, traction motor changing and general inspection. The locomotives are lifted on screw jacks.

On the extreme side of the shed adjacent to the fuelling point is a ground level wheel lathe capable of re-profiling an entire set of Class 58 tyres in just ten hours. The fuelling point itself has four fuelling positions, although only two locomotives can be fuelled at any one time, and takes its supply from tanks which can hold 150,000 gallons (682,000 litres) of fuel.

Although allocated only a few miles away at Toton, some Class 58s are stabled at Barrow Hill depot, where a number of drivers sign on duty, thus enabling the maximum work load to be obtained from each locomotive. Awaiting their next turns of duty at Barrow Hill on 6th April 1986 are Class 58 Nos 58041/002/020, in company with various Class 20 and 56 'Railfreight' machines.

Peter Gater

Operations

by Michael J. Collins BA

It was Thursday 9th December 1982 that the first Class 58 purpose-built freight locomotive was rolled out at the British Rail Engineering Limited (BREL) works at Doncaster which was her birthplace. Bedecked in the then new 'Railfreight' livery No. 58001 was placed on view to the public for the first time after a special ceremony in which it was driven through a plastic screen draped across the tracks. This launched the new 'Railfreight' enterprise and the new image for BR freight traffic which the marketing experts at BR wished to portray.

However its first outing on BR tracks was nearly two months later, when No. 58001 was towed south with engine running by Class 31 No. 31182 on Saturday 12th February to the Railway Technical Centre (RTC), Derby. Here a number of static tests were carried out, as was one riding trip to Bedford behind Class 45/1 No. 45106. Designated 1T21 the train comprised No. 58001 plus RTC test cars Nos 6, 10, and 11. The Class 58 again had its engine running, but the Class 45 was providing traction. After this outing the locomotive was sent to its new home, Toton (TO), and operated a couple of merry-go-round (MGR) coal trains, but saw little real action for some time. No. 58001 was dispatched to BREL Doncaster on 26th February for further braking tests.

On the morning of 31st March 1983 No. 58001 left Doncaster on a driver training run to Lincoln and return with a fully loaded MGR set. Three weeks later, on 21st April she had another outing, this time to Peterborough with a test train of eight Mk II coaches for a high speed trip along the East Coast Main Line, where a maximum speed of 79 mph was recorded. This was the first time a Class 58 locomotive had ever hauled passenger stock. It arrived in Peterborough station at 15.12 and returned north about an hour later. Eight days later on 29th April No. 58001 was noted at

The first outing for Class 58 No. 58001 was on 12th February 1983 when it was hauled by Class 31/1 No. 31182 from BREL Doncaster to the Railway Technical Centre. The ensemble complete with standard BR brake van are seen near Clay Cross Junction.
John Tuffs

Immingham Docks on another test working of MGR hoppers.

On 24th May 1983 the second locomotive, No. 58002 arrived at Toton depot for a start to be made on crew training. Early drivers in training noticed and remarked about the differences in cab comfort in relation to the 1970s designed Class 56s which they were used to.

The new locomotive was soon in the news because on 28th June it was used to supplement the two Class 31s on the 10.10 Corby – Lackenby 'Steeliner' between Corby and Toton – all in the name of driver training!

On 8th June 1983 No. 58003 made its commissioning run to Peterborough. The first recorded passenger working of a Class 58, occurred on 18th September 1983, when the "58 Pioneer" enthusiasts' special from Paddington to Matlock was operated by No. 58002 from Nuneaton to Matlock via Nottingham. A week earlier the same machine had been a visitor to the Midland Railway Centre, Butterley, to take part in an exhibition of traction and rolling stock.

Soon Class 58s were coming off the production line at Doncaster at the rate of about one a month. In January 1984 more crew training was taking place with No. 58005 at Saltley and No. 58006 at Bescot enabling Birmingham crews to be trained, and thus extending the locomotives' operating range. By 23rd February a Class member had reached the Cambridgeshire town of March on a revenue earning working, when No. 58012 was used in place of a failed locomotive on the 6G03 11.00 York – Whitemoor freight, later returning light locomotive to Doncaster. A possible first was the sight of No. 58007 plus dead Class 50 No. 50003 *Temeraire* noted passing Toton on 1st February 1984 en route from Doncaster Works.

By February 1984 class members were putting in appearances on Merseyside with export coal trains from East Midlands pits to Garston Docks, travelling via Stoke and Crewe. An early visitor was No. 58004 on 9th February when it worked the 15.30 Rawdon Colliery – Garston Dock service consisting of 30 HBA wagons, it returned later with the empties. Later in the month No. 58002 worked into Didcot Power Station with the 7Z64 09.55 Kingsbury – Didcot CEGB, and returned north with the 6Z64 empties, making the first Class 58 appearance on Western Region territory.

On 28th June 1983 the author made one of his first visits north in search of Class 58s in traffic, and was rewarded with this amazing sight of a triple header at Normanton-on-Soar, formed of Class 58 No. 58002 with Class 31s Nos 31224 and 31238 hauling the 10.10 Corby – Lackenby 'Steeliner'. The purpose of this super powered train was for Class 58 driver training.
Colin J. Marsden

During March No. 58019 was having problems leaving Doncaster, having had two attempts at operating test trains without success. The first one was cancelled by BREL when mechanical problems were discovered prior to departure and the second resulted in an ignominious failure at Grantham. The locomotive finally made a successful test on March 19th.

By now Class 58s were very familiar sights in the Birmingham area being used both on crew training and revenue earning duties from Bescot and Saltley on Rugeley – mid Cannock coal runs with occasional outings to Didcot Power Station. On 11th April 1984 No. 58014 arrived at Reading depot from Birmingham and stayed for nearly a month, being used on crew training duties, which included a trip to London's Old Oak Common on 3rd May, where it arrived light and departed with a rake of Mk II coaches bound for Oxford, forming a traction inspector's training trip. In the same month No. 58010 was being used thrice weekly working on crew training from Birmingham to Worcester via Kidderminster, staying for about an hour before returning. Meanwhile on 16th April No. 58008 had been noted working in multiple with Class 56 No. 56064 on

The first Class 58 to venture into the London division of the WR was No. 58014 on 3rd May 1984, when, in conjunction with traction training the locomotive operated light from Reading to Old Oak Common, from where it took a rake of Mk II's to Oxford. The locomotive is seen near West Ealing in this view.

Colin J. Marsden

Making one of the photographic sights of the year, No. 58002 slowly pulls round the curve at Cowley Bridge Junction near Exeter with a failed IC125 forming the 12.10 Liverpool – Penzance service on 1st September 1984, following the failure of the power cars in the Birmingham area.

David Mitchell

Heading the infamous Ashburys – Toton air braked freight. No. 58020 *Doncaster Works BRE* approaches Chinley on 10th April 1985 at the head of just four vehicles – two freight flats, and two Continental tank wagons.

John Tuffs

From February 1984 the Class 58s became a regular sight under the wires, at either the head of Rugeley MGR services or export coal trains bound for Garston. On 22nd July 1985 the first day of the 'new' Crewe layout. No. 58011 approaches the station with a Rawdon Colliery – Garston train.

Peter Gater

the daily Ratcliffe CEGB – Fletton (Peterborough) fly-ash train. The Class 58s were extending their range of operation in other directions too because on three consecutive days, 17–19th April No. 58002 powered the 4P51 12.13 Birmingham Lawley Street – Nottingham Freightliner and 4G50 15.23 return. This working occurred because of lack of coal work due to a dispute within the coal industry.

It was 9th July 1984 that saw the first visit of a Class 58 to Bristol. It was used to drag a failed Class 47, No. 47245 from the Birmingham area, and returned north immediately. A more spectacular visit occurred on 1st September, however, when 1V87 the 12.20 Liverpool Lime Street – Penzance HST failed in the Birmingham area with total loss of power on both power cars Nos. 43131/149. Widely quoted as the 'working of the year', the only available power at Birmingham was Class 58 No. 58002 which was placed at the head of the crippled HST and headed off west with a Saltley crew and various conductors. She passed Bristol, and still heading west, Taunton, Exeter, Newton Abbot, Totnes then further excitement! The 58 too failed – with brake pipe problems near Ivybridge and came to a complete stand – after some delay the rear power car was coaxed back into life and pushed the ensemble through to Plymouth, where the train was terminated by now some 90 minutes late. Having got the Class 58 to the West Country, Control then had the problem of getting it back. In the event it was hauled back to Bristol by Class 50 No. 50036 *Victorious* as far as Exeter and Class 31 No. 31202 onwards to Bristol. here Bath Road fitters managed to get the locomotive operating again, and the machine went back to Birmingham under its own power.

More passenger work followed on 16th September 1984 but this time only on a rail tour, No. 58007 was used on the ''Midland Macedoine'' enthusiasts' special which originated at St Pancras and featured Class 58 haulage from

On a bitterly cold 19th February 1985 No. 58018 approaches the site of the closed Trowell station, which shut its doors for the last time on 2nd January 1967, at the head of 11.20 Bennerley open cast site – Staythorpe working.

Colin J. Marsden

Derby to Sinfin, Buxton and return to Derby via Stoke-on-Trent.

The end of summer 1984 saw increased use of Class 58s on the southern half of the West Coast Main Line. For example No. 58012 worked the 7E63 Four Ashes – Ripple Lane freight as far as Willesden where it ran light back to Northampton to pick up a freight for Bescot. Crews from Bescot frequently gave a Class 58 a run down to London at this time by running light to Willesden to pick up the 16.43 Dover – Bescot 'Speedlink' which they took back under the wires with diesel haulage!

After a number of previous exploratory visits, regular workings of Class 58s into the Manchester area began in September 1984. A favourite working being the 08.43 Toton – Arpley 'Speedlink' as far as Ashburys, and the balancing 12.46 Ashburys – Toton which both worked over the scenic Hope Valley route. These trains produced extremely small loadings and it was common to see a massive Class 58 working with just one or two wagons. Inevitably the operating authorities deemed the working to be uneconomic and it was withdrawn the following year.

An exhibition held at Steamport, Southport led to the visit of No. 58010 to Springs Branch, Wigan so that it could be cleaned for display. A very unusual duty for a Class 58 was the 6M25 05.15 Stoke Gifford – Wolverton ARC stone train which occurred on 19th October 1984, when No. 58001 replaced the usual two Class 37s or Class 56, which are normally rostered for this duty. Another oddity occurred on 29th October when Class 56 No. 56039 failed near Slough on the 08.50 Brentford – Appleford refuse train and Class 58 No. 58011 was sent light from Didcot to assist.

During the Christmas/New Year period of 1984/5 the Ratcliffe-on-Soar to Fletton fly-ash trains were double-headed Class 58s – one of the first regular bookings. During the period 24th December – 1st January Nos. 58009/16 were used virtually every day (excepting Christmas Day and Boxing Day). The reason given by BR was that Toton depot was virtually shut down over the whole holiday period and the prospect of a single Class 58 failure was not to be contemplated. The double heading was therefore a form of insurance, and has been repeated in subsequent years.

Once sufficient train crews at Toton had been trained on their new charges, the daily CEGB Ratcliffe Power Station – Fletton fly-ash train commenced with Class 58 operation, replacing Class 56 hitherto used. However in 1987, although booked for a Class 58, various classes were regularly recorded. On 8th August 1985 No. 58015 is seen near Melton Mowbray bound for Fletton.

Michael J. Collins

Early 1984 saw the commencement of Class 58s on some Didcot CEGB workings, which at that time numbered some 20 per day, however by 1987 following various NCB, and BR industrial disputes where coal was transferred to road haulage and not won back by the railway, the daily schedule was down to around five. On 12th June 1985 the 11.14 Baddesley – Didcot is seen passing the closed but still existent Aynho station headed by No. 58029.

Colin J. Marsden

Above: To capture a Class 58 and 59 in the same frame is somewhat rare, but quite remarkable when the location is Toton Depot. No. 58033 is seen hauling Class 59 No. 59003 away from the shed building on 17th October 1987 when the Yeoman locomotive was at the depot for technical observation.

Simon Hartshorne

Below: With another heavy load of coal bound for CEGB Willington Power Station, No. 58047 approaches Clay Cross Junction on 18th September 1987 with a morning service from Markham Colliery.

Colin J. Marsden

The use of Class 58s on anything but MGR trains has always brought the photographers out, one train which often produced a Class 58, but ceased to operate in Spring 1987 was the Birmingham (Lawley Street) – Nottingham and return Freightliner service, which utilised a member of the class if one was spare at Saltley. No. 58014 is seen on the 15.21 Nottingham – Lawley Street on 5th July 1984 near Burton-on-Trent.

John Tuffs

The first ever visit of a Class 58 to Healey Mills came on 29th January 1985 when No. 58017 arrived on a 'Freightliner' from the Sheffield direction. On the previous day No. 58012 made an unexpected sight at York with a Tinsley – Lackenby steel diagram. A similar train five months later on 7th May produced No. 58011.

During March 1985 tests were undertaken by the Railway Technical Centre at Derby on Class 58 bogies. In connection with this Nos. 58004/005 made several runs in the Nottingham/Derby area coupled one either end of test car No. 6 (ADB975290), the pair also worked the Ratcliffe – Fletton fly-ash duty with the test car coupled between them on a few occasions. The MEE was conducting tests because of a continued problem with wheel slip/slide under certain rail conditions.

On 5th May 1985 No. 58002 was exhibited at an Open Day held at Westbury down yard, this being the first reported Class 58 at the Wiltshire town.

Spring fever hit Class 58s early in 1985 after they seemed to develop an affinity for London terminal stations. The first sighting was at Paddington when No. 58003 turned up on the 19.17 from Birmingham New Street, after the failure of the rostered train locomotive at Coventry on 24th April. Less than a month later, on 11th May No. 58011 appeared at Euston with the 01.15 Holyhead (the "Irish Mail") which had been diverted via Banbury and Reading due to a Freightliner derailment at Watford Junction. It returned north on the 10.20 Euston – Stranraer which it worked as far as Birmingham.

No. 58029 was a spectacular visitor to Newport (Gwent) on 8th June when, in brand new condition, it hauled the 4V73 19.00 Newcastle – Pengam Freightliner. On the same day No. 58013 was exhibited at Aylesbury as part of a 'Rail Week' event.

On 28th June the Class was really breaking unusual ground when No. 58001 was the first of the type to traverse the Skelton Junction (Manchester) – Arpley Junction (Warrington) line with a Toton – Garston export coal train. No doubt it was one of the last visitors of the class to the line, as the route closed completely on 8th July 1985.

On 14th July 1985 No. 58030 (then the latest in traffic) was exhibited at an Open Day held at the Midland Railway Centre, Butterley. Then on 17th July No. 58019 arrived at Llandudno Junction on a crew training trip from Crewe, returning eastwards to Cheshire immediately. This training was in connection with projected Class 58s on additional export coal trains.

By mid September 1985 Class 58s gained a regular turn which took them on the Southern Region, when they commenced operation to the Blue Circle Industries works at Northfleet, with MGR trains from Silverhill Colliery. On 29th December 1985 No. 58005 was noted at the works with a rake of 41 HAA hoppers, with No. 58006 arriving the following day.

On 9th January 1986 No. 58039 arrived at Carlisle under the control of a Toton crew with a special MGR train which it worked throughout from the East Midlands, owing to the lack of a spare engine at Crewe. This visit to the border town was followed by another on 19th July 1986 when No. 58017 arrived for the open day event to be held at Upperby depot partnering failed Class 86/2 No. 86244 with an empty stock train.

At this time 'new build' locomotives were being delayed at Doncaster Works due to the non-availability of certain essential components. The delivery of Nos. 58038-40 was therefore not completed until early March when the missing parts were manufactured. Meanwhile, availability of completed examples of the class was also low because of a spate of piston fractures which made necessary unscheduled trips to BREL Doncaster for repair.

Although Class 58s regularly worked into the Scunthorpe area on test runs from Doncaster it was as late as 2nd April 1986 that one appeared in revenue earning service at the British Steel coal handling plant. Honours were performed by No. 58013 which worked in on an MGR which originated from Betteshanger Colliery in Kent, however the Class 58 only operated the train from Toton.

Early Summer 1986 saw a Class 58 pressed into service on passenger trains. On 7th June No. 58037 was used to relieve Class 47 No. 47558 on the 06.52 Leeds – Poole from

The Shirebrook based MGR operations were some of the last to see regular Class 58 haulage, and it was not until 1986 that large numbers were reported in the area. After a slight snowfall No. 58007 passes Shirebrook Junction with an empty MGR set bound for Shirebrook Colliery on 20th February 1986.

John Tuffs

Birmingham to Reading, the locomotive was then used to take the 11.40 (Saturday only) Poole – Liverpool from Reading throughout to Liverpool, achieving its maximum speed of 80 mph several times and arriving at Oxford early! The locomotive returned to Birmingham with the 19.05 Liverpool Lime Street – Paddington. Just over a month later on 26th July No. 58025 worked the 08.40 Liverpool – Paignton from Birmingham New Street to Bristol, after the failure of the double headed Class 31/4s, the stock on this train being the Mk III Pullmans.

On 20th September 1986 a Class 58 was again at the head of Pullman stock when No. 58039 operated the "Lincolnshire Coast Pullman" railtour from King's Cross to Skegness and Cleethorpes. This also brought the first Class 58 into King's Cross.

By late 1986 the Shirebrook MGR turns were almost entirely in the hands of Class 58s. On three occasions at the beginning of the year the class re-acquainted itself with March, on 11th February and again on 17th February No. 58020 arrived after working the Washwood Heath – Harwich Town car train re-routed because of problems on the North London Line. On 12th February No. 58039 was entrusted with the same train.

Meanwhile in January a Class 58 had been seen towing an HST set again when the 11.00 King's Cross – Edinburgh was declared a total failure at Doncaster. The defective unit was towed away to Neville Hill depot for repair. During late March No. 58001 was reported operating in the Blackpool area on ecs duties. A few days prior, on 10th March No. 58005 operated a Tinsley – Cardiff Tidal Sidings special steel train throughout and worked back north on the booked Tidal Sidings – Washwood Heath ABS freight.

The final member of the Class, No. 58050 although completed in January 1987 did not enter revenue earning service until the end of the year, as the locomotive was fitted with experimental 'Sepex' modifications. On 2nd April it ran the Peterborough test train but failed near Retford, and had to be assisted back to Doncaster by Class 56 No. 56014. Two days later she had been repaired and was transferred to Derby and the test track at Old Dalby for active testing by both BR and Brush. No. 58050 did not join the others of the build at Toton until mid July.

This brings the Class 58 story to date, always associated with MGR and heavy freight traffic, members of the class are appearing sporadically on other traffic and in many parts of the country. With a life expectancy which will see them in service well into the next century no doubt they will be seen, in time, in virtually all parts of the country.

Hauling a heavy load of coal away from Warsop Junction on 18th September 1987 No. 58023 traverses the single line while in charge of a Welbeck Colliery – CEGB West Burton duty.

Colin J. Marsden

Namings

by Michael J. Collins & Michael J.
Richardson

There is no doubt that the act of bestowing a name on a locomotive gives the selected machine a little extra piquancy and interest for the average railway enthusiast. The sight of a named locomotive is so much more memorable than the sight of a more mundane example not graced with a name and bearing only a number as a means of identification. Indeed, rail enthusiasts will flock in their hundreds when a naming ceremony is announced in order to see the curtains drawn back to reveal the nameplate. For the general travelling public too, there is something a little more grand when, after waiting patiently for a train's arrival, one notices that haulage is to be by a locomotive bearing a name. Somehow that little nameplate gives the locomotive a facet of extra identity which lifts it from obscurity to fix it in the minds of all sections of the travelling public.

The pre-grouping railway companies certainly recognised the above phenomenon and vast numbers of steam locomotives, even in early BR days, were graced with a name. Later, a large number of the pilot scheme diesels bore a name but unfortunately, during the mid-1960s a 'no-naming' policy was instigated by BR in the interests of cultivating a 'corporate image' for its traction fleet. This ban lasted for 10 years but happily, was lifted in 1975 when naming of passenger locomotives recommenced. The decision to again name locomotives can be attributed to the more publicity orientated approach then being portrayed by Sir Peter Parker, the then Chairman of British Rail. With the aid of the mass media and the immediacy afforded by publicity gained on television and radio, BR quickly came to realise the value of naming locomotives. They noted the high value in the exercise both in terms of increased cash receipts and the more nebulous, but equally important value, of good public relations. During the late 1970s and early 1980s a veritable flood of namings of all types of locomotives took place in order to cash in on the positive effects that had been identified.

Financial restraints imposed by the Government in the early 1980s forced a re-think, however, because there was no doubt that the fitting of nameplates to locomotives, coupled with all the attendant razzmatazz was an expensive business. One solution was to get certain bodies, eg local District Councils, to pay for their own nameplates and their fitment costs. Another was the opinion which grew out of BR Marketing to the effect that very positive financial effects can be gained from fitting nameplates bearing a link with prestigious companies – thus, the naming policy has been skewed in recent years because BR has come to recognise that within the sphere of its overall finances the movement of freight is a vital money-earner. Not only do passengers need encouragement to keep using BR but freight customers too need coaxing to part with their hard earned money within a competitive and quite cut-throat marketing environment. BR came to realise that the dedication of individual locomotives to certain traffic flows not only lead to increased pride and care by their own staff, but also lead to very positive benefits from within their customers' camps. A locomotive which bears a customer's name and, day in day out, hauls the same customer's traffic, was seen as an important marketing ploy and one which could well not only attract freight traffic to BR but also have the added benefit of retaining traffic already won.

This is the context in which one must view the naming

On the day of the Class 58 launch at Doncaster No. 58001 had the dubious honour of being named *Railfreight*. However as all other Class 58s carry the same embellishment, as do a number of other locomotive classes, this can hardly be accurately called a locomotive 'naming'. The illustration shows the curtains being unveiled over the 'Railfreight' name by Mr. H. Sanderson, then BR's Freight Director.

Colin J. Marsden

So as to fit the *Doncaster Works BRE* plate, the 'Railfreight' logo had to be repositioned slightly higher than usual. The plates fitted to No. 58020 whilst acceptable to most were not to the liking of the BREL management, who on the day of naming were disgusted to find the BRE legend picked out in light blue. Such was the controversy surrounding this that in Spring 1987 new plates were cast omitting the BRE legend. The revised plates were then fitted in a central position as the 'Railfreight' logo was applied as a casting to the front end.

Colin J. Marsden

of the Class 58s. Hailed from design stage as purpose-built freight locomotives; focussed in-service on coal sub-sector traffic, it is only natural in the present naming climate that several of the locomotives have names applied which reflect both the coal and the power industries.

Paradoxically, in view of the importance given by BR to naming ceremonies, the first naming of a Class 58, No.58001 turned out in retrospect to be a little of a fraud. At about noon on 9th December 1982 No. 58001 was rolled out of Doncaster Works for its first public showing. With predictable panache a naming ceremony took place when red plastic 'Railfreight' stickers fitted under the cab windows were unveiled by Henry Sanderson, then BR's Freight Director. We now know that No. 58001 was the first of many locomotives to carry these name stickers and therefore the locomotive was not really named at all. A naming ceremony did take place however, and so for the purposes of this work the occasion has to be recorded. Prior to the applied style other variations had been tried, including 'Railfreight' in black on the yellow background, as well as being evaluated in white on a black background. Both schemes were rejected as non-eyecatching.

Corporate style nameplate as applied to No. 58039 *Rugeley Power Station*. Note the CEGB logo applied in the top left corner.
Colin J. Marsden

The first official Class 58 naming came on 7th November 1984, when No. 58020 received the name *Doncaster Works BRE* at BREL Doncaster, again Mr. H. Sanderson performed the honours, who is seen in this illustration pointing to the plate. On the dias with Mr. Sanderson, were the Doncaster Works Manager, and the BREL Managing Director.
Colin J. Marsden

To promote BR's association with other industry, several Class 58s have been given nameplates of major Railfreight customers. On 6th September 1986 No. 58041 was named *Ratcliffe Power Station* in a ceremony held at the power station. The locomotive is seen posed in the grounds on display.

J. Wheeler

Nameplate as fitted to No. 58041 *Ratcliffe Power Station*, CEGB logo in top left corner.

J. Wheeler

Name *Cottam Power Station* as carried by locomotive No. 58040.

Michael J. Collins

Class 58s had been around for almost two years before any were adorned with cast nameplates. Twenty-three months and 20 locomotives into the build, the then brand new No. 58020 was named *Doncaster Works BRE* by Henry Sanderson, Freight Director, on 7th November 1984 at Doncaster Works. Also in attendance were Geoff James, BREL Manufacturing Director, and Derek Clarke, Doncaster Works Manager. The locomotive was named in recognition of over 130 years of locomotive building at Doncaster. BR picked Doncaster's 2,512th locomotive to carry the name. The plates themselves were 1,309 mm wide (now standard for Class 58) by 450 mm deep. The lettering was of the usual type, polished on a red background, except for the 'BRE' which was slightly smaller and raised on a blue background. The plates were positioned low down on the cab sides, below the 'Railfreight' emblem, which was now fixed directly under the driver's assistant's window. However, changing circumstances led to changing names. In the second half of 1986 it was announced that BREL were to relinquish their total hold at Doncaster and BR were to take over the maintenance operation.

This would mean that the Doncaster flagship would be slightly inaccurate, so in August 1986 No. 58020 received new nameplates of the same dimensions but omitting the BRE logo. Re-naming was done without ceremony.

Operations of Class 58s began in the Nottinghamshire coalfield area centred on Shirebrook depot from Autumn 1985. On 12th December 1985 No. 58034 was named *Bassetlaw* (the name of the local District Council) to mark the link between this type of locomotive and the tight-knit mining communities in the area. The naming ceremony was held at Worksop, unveiling being performed by Councillor Dennis Wells, then Chairman of Bassetlaw Council. No. 58034 being selected because it was the newest Class 58 in traffic at the time. The plates for this locomotive measure 998 mm by 250 mm and, to date, are the smallest carried on a Class 58. Unlike No. 58020 the 'Railfreight' emblem appears below the nameplate, which is centrally positioned on the cab side. A small plaque of Bassetlaw District Council is centrally mounted above the name. The name-plates for this particular machine were cast by David Newton – owner of the famous Newton Replica business, which now fabricates most BR nameplates and provides replicas to railway enthusiasts.

During September 1986 a quartet of Class 58s were named during special Open Day events held at CEGB power stations in recognition of the large volume of rail borne traffic carried for this customer. The first naming was No. 58041 *Ratcliffe Power Station* which was named on 6th September. The naming ceremony was conducted by Deputy Chairman and Production Director of the CEGB, Mr. Gil Blackman. The plates were the same size as for No. 58020 but the top left hand corner incorporated the CEGB 'Electric E' logo, which is a blue 'E' on a white square background. The plate was mounted centrally on the cab side, with no 'Railfreight' emblem. Instead, BR had produced cast 'nameplates' bearing the legend 'Railfreight' which was attached to the centre of each cab front.

The following Saturday, 13th September, Rugeley CEGB held an Open Day, and No. 58039 was named *Rugeley Power Station*. The nameplates being of the same dimensions as on No. 58041 and again the 'Railfreight' cast plates were applied to the front.

On 20th September, No. 58040 was named *Cottam Power Station* at Cottam, which is 10 kms east of Retford. On the following Saturday, 27th September, No. 58042 was named *Ironbridge Power Station*. All four sets of plates bear the CEGB logo in the corner and locomotives carry their 'Railfreight' plaques on the front.

On 14th March 1987 No. 58049 became the second BR locomotive to bear the name of a British coalmine (the first being a Class 56 named *Taff Merthyr*). The Class 58 was named *Littleton Colliery* at the Colliery which is located near Cannock, Staffordshire, by the Mine Manager, Mr. Blakeley. The plate was of a new design featuring the British Coal logo written in small block capitals within a rectangle at the top of the plate.

Saturday 9th May 1987 saw Toton TMD opened to its staff and their families for a private Open Day. Highlight of the day was the naming of No. 58050 *Toton Traction Depot* in recognition of the exclusively Railfreight Sector Depot which has amongst its allocation the entire Class 58 fleet. In attendance at the ceremony were Mr. Leslie Smith from Railfreight, Cyril Bleasdale LM General Manager, and Brian Harris, Area Maintenance Engineer, Toton. At the time of the naming No. 58050 was under evaluation for its 'SEPEX' fitting and was returned to the Railway Technical Centre, Derby. On 18th September 1987 prior to No. 58050 ever operating a revenue earning train, it was sent minus its nameplates to Stratford Major Depot for repainting into the new Railfreight Sector livery. Its temporary de-naming was to allow the names to be stripped and ceramically treated with black letters on a yellow background. However after completion this was deemed as not acceptable and the names were retreated to appear on the locomotive at its official launch on 15th October with polished metal letters on a matt black background. The 'Railfreight' plates were similarly treated and against official instructions re-applied to the front end.

The casting of the nameplates for this fleet has been done by two parties: BREL Swindon dealing with the plates for Nos 58020 (both sets), Nos 58039-42 and No. 58049; whilst Newton Replicas have cast those for Nos 58034 and 58050 together with all the 'Railfreight' plates.

Under normal practise three plates are cast for each locomotive, two to be applied and one for presentational purposes. If additional plates are required for a locomotive, due to accident or theft, a new mould has to be formed.

And what in the future? At the time of writing three plates have been cast for a Class 58 to be named *Daw Mill Colliery*, which is situated mid-way between Water Orton and Nuneaton on the Birmingham-Leicester line. These plates are of the standard format and finished in black, which are scheduled to be applied to a sector liveried locomotive in the near future.

Above: Although No. 58050 was named *Toton Traction Depot* in the summer of 1987, the nameplates were removed during the second week of September when the locomotive was selected to be repainted in the new sector colours. No. 58050 devoid of plates poses outside Stratford major depot on 22nd September.

Brian Morrison

Below: Bassetlaw No. 58034 carries both its name and a Railfreight sticker under the driver's assistant's side window. Although intended to carry a cast frontal 'Railfreight' plate, this fitment is now unlikely to be fitted because, as locomotives undergo classified attention, new Railfreight, sub-sector colours will be applied which do not cater for the 'Railfreight' legend. On 11th February 1988 No. 58034 approaches Stenson Junction with a trip for CEGB Willington.

Colin J. Marsden

In Detail

Class 58 front end layout. 1– Warning horns (behind grille). 2– Red tail indicator light, 3– White front marker light, 4– High intensity headlight, 5– Multiple control jumper cable (red diamond), 6– Multiple control jumper receptacle (red diamond), 7– Locomotive control air pipe, 8– Air brake pipe, 9– Main reservoir pipe, 10– Coupling, 11– Snowplough brackets. Locomotive illustrated is No. 58042.

Colin J. Marsden

Body side detail of original design Class 58 without compartment door handles. The between bogie equipment consists of battery box, fuel tank and brake equipment.

Colin J. Marsden

Cab side and bogie detail of No. 2 end, driver's side, giving detail of CP3 bogie arrangement, and louvre doors over electrical equipments.

Colin J. Marsden

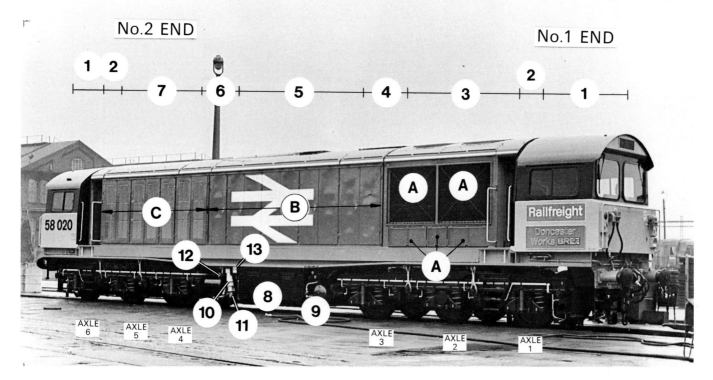

Class 58 side detail – Right hand side. 1– Cab module, 2– Transverse walkway, 3– Radiator or cooler module, 4– Air compressor and drive shaft compartment, 5– Power unit compartment, 6– Alternator, Turbo charger and Engine air intake filter compartment, 7– Clean air compartment housing electrical equipment and brake modules, 8– Battery boxes with fuel tank behind, 9– Air reservoir, 10– Fuel transfer pump, 11– Fire bottle (behind pump), 12– Fuel intake, 13– Fire pull handle. The locomotive illustrated is No. 58020.

Colin J. Marsden

Class 58 side detail – Left hand side. 1– Cab module, 2– Transverse walkway, 3– Radiator or cooler group, 4– Air compressor and drive shaft compartment, 5– Power unit compartment, 6– Alternator, Turbo charger and Engine air intake filter compartment, 7– Clean air compartment housing electrical equipment and brake modules, 8– Battery boxes with fuel tank behind, 9– Battery isolating switch, 10– Air reservoir, 11– Fire pull handle. The locomotive illustrated is No. 58022.

Colin J. Marsden

LEFT HAND SIDE

Only relatively minor mishaps have befallen the Class 58 fleet, and at the time of writing no module changes have been effected. On 23rd August 1984 No. 58008 became derailed at Tibshelf Sidings, Westhouses, after working through incorrectly set points. Rerailing was effected by the Toton 75ton crane later in the day. Fitters are seen positioning the lifting slings around the bogie, prior to lifting the No. 1 end.

S. Freeman

At a number of locations catch points are provided to protect running lines from other operating lines or sidings. These are always protected by signals, but if for some reason a driver passes the signal at danger he may well find himself (and his locomotive) quickly 'off the track', as was the case at Peterborough on 2nd August 1985 when No. 58030 derailed on catch points at the north end of the station. At the time the locomotive was less than eight weeks old!

John Rudd

One of the most serious accidents to befall a Class 58 was on 20th November 1986 when No. 58019 hauling an afternoon Coalville – Rugeley MGR collided with a south bound steel train at Branston Junction near Burton-on-Trent. Although derailing all wheels, and ending up at a very undignified angle, no serious locomotive damage occurred, although the Class 31 on the steel train suffered serious side damage and cost over £100,000 to repair. The upper photograph shows the locomotive's position after the collision, while the lower picture shows the locomotive some two days after the derailment. Note the missing buffer and underframe damage, which were repaired at Toton depot.

Both: John Tuffs

In Traffic

To observe Class 58s on anything apart from MGR duties on the Erewash Valley line is quite unusual, however on 14th August 1984 the photographer was lucky enough to capture this view of No. 58009 approaching Trowell Junction with a train of loaded 'Sealion' ballast hoppers.

John Tuffs

With a rake of 41 empty HAA wagons in tow, No. 58023 approaches Trowell Junction on 19th February 1985 bound for Silverhill Colliery. After loading, the train returned to Ratcliffe Power Station. During a 24 hour cycle a formation such as this could make three round trips between the power station and colliery.

Colin J. Marsden

With the remnants of some snow still laying, No. 58023 (see previous illustration) approaches Trowell Junction with a Silverhill Colliery – Ratcliffe CEGB working on 19th February 1985.

Colin J. Marsden

The Erewash Valley line is of four track section throughout, but traffic levels are very light, and it would not come as a surprise to learn that some sort of rationalisation is to take place. Photographed north of the site of Ilkeston station No. 58032 heads for Sutton Colliery with an empty MGR rake on 2nd May 1986.

Colin J. Marsden

With the splendid Great Northern, Derby Friargate – Nottingham line viaduct at Ilkeston as a backdrop, ex works No. 58024 heads along the up slow line with the 7T47 trip from Sutton Colliery to Willington Power Station on 18th February 1985. The coal loading equipment behind the viaduct is that of Bennerley open cast site.
Colin J. Marsden

Although the GN viaduct at Ilkeston is officially sealed off to the public, access is possible and provides a splendid panoramic view of the Erewash Valley line. No. 58023 crosses from the down main line to the Bennerley disposal point on 12th May 1986 with the usual rake of merry-go-round hoppers.
John Tuffs

The Bennerley disposal point, which was only modernised to accommodate MGR type trains in the early 1980s, sees some three workings per day, which are powered by a mixture of Class 56 and 58 locomotives. Emerging from the small complex, No. 58013 heads for Ratcliffe Power Station on 20th March 1985.

John Tuffs

A short distance north of Ilkeston is Shipley Gate, which also had a thriving station, but this was closed on 27th August 1948. The track layout still shows the tell-tale signs that there was once a station, nearly 40 years later. On 19th February 1985 No. 58009 approaches Shipley Gate on the up main line with a Silverhill – Willington trip (7T49).

Colin J. Marsden

One of the rarest Class 58s to photograph has been No. 58014, as during its short career it spent the period August 1986 – July 1987 at Doncaster Works, where it was used as a 'Christmas Tree', supplying other locomotives with spare parts. On 19th February 1985 the locomotive was captured passing Shipley Gate on a Ratcliffe bound working.

Colin J. Marsden

Passing the site of the former Codnor Park and Ironville station, closed under the Beeching reign in 1967, No. 58006 heads for one of the North Derbyshire pits on 19th August 1985 with empty hoppers from CEGB Ratcliffe Power Station.

John Tuffs

During the course of the day some 50 MGR trains are diagrammed to traverse the Erewash Valley line, however with daily alterations, depending on specific power station requirements and colliery output figures, the actual trains are often hard to trace. On 19th August 1985 No. 58012 passes Codnor Park with a Ratcliffe duty.

John Tuffs

The only semi regular Class 58 on a freightliner train has been the Birmingham Lawley Street – Nottingham, and return duty, which regrettably ceased to operate from April 1987. On 3rd May 1984 the return working, headed by No. 58009 is seen near Burton-on-Trent.

John Tuffs

The booked formation for the Nottingham freightliner was just one 5-set, which, as illustrated was normally well loaded. No. 58014 nears Wichnor Junction, south of Burton on the North East – South West route on a sunny 6th July 1984 with the 15.21 Nottingham – Lawley Street.

John Tuffs

The line between Sheet Stores Junction, and Stenson Junction is freight only, and sees a number of trains each day, one train being the Nottingham freightliner. On 8th June 1984 it is seen at Barrow-on-Trent with No. 58013 providing the motive power.

John Tuffs

No. 58015 was barely a month old when photographed passing the site of the former Branston station, south of Burton on 26th October 1984, while hauling the 15.21 Nottingham – Lawley Street service, on one of the few occasions that the formation was strengthened to ten vehicles.

John Tuffs

On a number of occasions the Lawley Street – Southampton freightliner has produced a Class 58, but usually only as far as Oxford or Reading, the train only being recorded once to operate onto the SR with the 58 still at the helm. On 27th April 1985 No. 58013 passes under the wires at Berkswell with the Southampton bound service.

Michael J. Collins

The area around Harbury, south of Leamington Spa on the GW route to Birmingham provides some splendid photographic view points. Traversing Harbury Cutting on 26th May 1984 Class 58 No. 58009 powers the Southampton – Lawley Street working, formed of two 5-set freightliners.

Michael J. Collins

North of Banbury is the village of Cropredy, which until September 1956 had a station, and today sees a regular procession of Class 58s, on the diagrammed Didcot MGRs, or making their infrequent appearances on Southampton freightliner workings. On 25th July 1987 when this illustration was taken, the horse in the field was more interested in the photographer than in Class 58 No. 58047 powering the Southampton freightliner.

John C. Baker

The fourth member of the Class 58 fleet, which entered service in September 1983 is seen near Cropredy on 18th August 1984 with the Lawley Street – Southampton train. This train is driven by Saltley crews, who are the only men in the area trained on the their operation.

John C. Baker

Around Burton

The area around Burton-on-Trent sees a considerable amount of Class 58 activity, usually at the head of MGR traffic. Fortunately for the photographer a number of suitable overbridges are conveniently located to vary the illustrations. No. 58006 is seen near Wetmore on 4th September 1986 with a Didcot CEGB – Toton Old Bank empty MGR working.

John Tuffs

With the inevitable tea can in the assistant driver's window, No. 58013 is seen near Burton-on-Trent on 23rd July 1985 with a loaded Rawdon Colliery – Willington Power Station working. Sets on this duty are normally formed of 36 hopper rakes.

John Tuffs

Again near Wetmore is this illustration of No. 58030 on 1st November 1985 on train number 6F99, empties from Willington CEGB bound for Rawdon Colliery on the Coalville line. On the far left of the illustration is Wetmore sidings signal box.

John Tuffs

The area around Stenson Junction, north of Burton also sees a high proportion of Class 58 activity, with all the Burton line services, and in addition, any traffic taking the Crewe line, or arriving at CEGB Willington Power Station from the North. Passing Stenson Junction on 10th July 1986 No. 58038 heads an export coal train bound for Garston Docks formed of just 19 MGR vehicles.

Colin J. Marsden

Travelling at walking pace as it approaches Willington CEGB Power Station No. 58046 brings in some 2,500 tonnes of coal from the Denby Opencast site on 1st May 1987. Note the air brake fitted brake van coupled behind the locomotive.

John Tuffs

It is very unusual to find Class 58s double heading, and many of those recorded are due to failures, or for balancing purposes. On 18th June 1986 an additional 'Steeliner' from Corby to Lackenby is seen approaching Toton with Nos 58008/035 at the head. It is understood that this pairing was due to balancing of traction.

Peter Gater

After suffering an apparent failure, No. 58006 is piloted by sister locomotive No. 58016 on a Drakelow – Coalville empty MGR working on 26th September 1986, seen passing Swains Park and approaching Moira West.

John Tuffs

Above: Class 58 No. 58034 *Bassetlaw* is seen piloting Class 56 No. 56019 at Codnor Park on the Erewash Valley line on 15th May 1987 in charge of 6T46, a Ratcliffe CEGB – Bentinck Colliery empty MGR duty. The Class 56 had suffered a failure, and the Class 58 summoned to assist, later removing the failed Class 56 to TO depot for repair.

John Tuffs

As detailed in the 'Operations Section' text, the Ratcliffe – Fletton fly-ash workings are usually doubleheaded over the Christmas/New Year period as a safeguard against locomotive failure. On 27th December 1984 the Ratcliffe – Fletton working 6E51 is seen arriving at Fletton behind Nos 58009/16.

John Rudd

Right: With both locomotives operating, a total of 6,600 bhp is available, quite adequate to shift the Fletton bound fly-ash working seen entering the Fletton brick complex headed by Nos 58009/16, again on 29th December 1984.

John Rudd

Left: Sporting its cast 'Railfreight' plate on the front end No. 58040 *Cottam Power Station* pilots Class 56 No. 56063 *Bardon Hill* on an unidentified north bound empty MGR train approaching Toton on 6th February 1987. Again the reason given for this double heading was a failure of the train locomotive.

John Tuffs

Didcot Bound

The Class 58s commenced operating Didcot MGR services in February 1984, following the training of Birmingham area train crews. Passing under the elevated section of the M6 Motorway near Bromford Bridge, No. 58025 heads the 10.15 Bagworth – Didcot on 8th October 1985.

John Tuffs

The supply of coal to Didcot emulates from a number of Derbyshire, Leicestershire, Nottinghamshire and other Midland pits, and during 1984-85 there were upwards of 20 trains per day. On 4th June 1985 No. 58018 passes Cropredy near Banbury with a Birch Coppice – Didcot working.

John Tuffs

Following various industrial disputes and a reorganisation within the NCB, much of the coal for Didcot now arrives by road, which would equate to 50 juggernauts on our roads to just one train! On 23rd April 1985 a very clean No. 58025 is seen near King's Sutton, heading for Didcot.

John Tuffs

When the Didcot traffic was more prolific during 1985, a number of photographers made 'trips' to the Didcot – Birmingham line where they could be sure of netting about 25 exposures during the daylight hours. With the village of King's Sutton in the background No. 58010 heads north with the 17.15 Didcot – Kingsbury empty MGR on 12th June 1985.

Colin J. Marsden

Train consists of between 30-40 MGR hoppers are the norm for Didcot duties, depending on the originating point of the train. Heading a 30 vehicle set on 12th June 1985, No. 58023 nears Aynho Junction with the 14.40 Didcot – Mantle Lane (Coalville) empties.

Colin J. Marsden

Today most MGR operations are single manned, whereby the train is under the sole control of the driver, brake tests and train preparation being carried out by terminal staff. No. 58029 approaches the now closed Aynho station with the 15.55 Didcot – Barrow Hill.

Colin J. Marsden

A number of semaphore signals still exist in the Aynho area, giving the photographer something interesting other than the train to include in his photograph. Passing the down line home signal near Aynho Junction, No. 58026 approaches the Junction with a Didcot bound duty on 23rd April 1985, when the locomotive was just four weeks out of Doncaster Works.

John Tuffs

Although closed to passengers unfortunately, the northbound station building at Aynho still exists, used today by a local coal merchant. With the tail of its train just clearing the Bicester line flyover, No. 58018 heads south with the 13.57 Barrow Hill – Didcot of 12th June 1985.

Colin J. Marsden

The area around Heyford provides some splendid photographic viewpoints, and in several areas both trains and the canal can be captured in the same picture. With the South Oxfordshire canal on the right, No. 58023 passes Heyford station with a Barrow Hill – Didcot working.

Colin J. Marsden

By 1987 the bookings for Didcot MGRs were down to around five per day, and on several occasions in the summer, some of these were cancelled. This dearth of rail movement has not only put yet more traffic onto our roads, but must have placed some of the motive power departments jobs in jeopardy. A loaded MGR set is seen near Heyford with the 09.40 Barrow Hill – Didcot of 12th June 1985.

Brian Morrison

If the need arose Didcot CEGB could accommodate five trains at the same time, but this is unlikely to ever occur. On 27th March 1985 No. 58010 awaits admittance to the discharging equipment in one of the reception roads, with a train of 40 hoppers.

Colin J. Marsden

When the train passes through the automatic discharge equipment the driver utilises the slow speed control (SSC) equipment, whereby the speed of the train is kept constant at a pre-determined level by the locomotive's electronics. No. 58010 slowly passes through the discharge shed. Note the speed control signals either side of the two tracks, which are operated by the power station control room.

Brian Morrison

If all goes well during the discharging process a train can arrive and be ready to depart from Didcot in around one hour, however due to the distance between power station and colliery only one 'trip' can be made during a driver's duty. On 27th March 1985 No. 58011 slowly departs from the discharging area and awaits clearance onto the main line.

Brian Morrison

After departing the CEGB complex, the train passes through Foxhall Junction, and Didcot North Junction to gain the GW Brimingham route. Photographed on the freight only curve near Foxhall Junction No. 58011 heads back to the Midlands on 27th March 1985.

Colin J. Marsden

With the Great Western Society (Didcot) complex in the background an empty MGR rake awaits the signal at Didcot North Junction to join the Didcot avoiding line, and head towards Oxford.

Colin J. Marsden

On the rare occasion a Class 58 has operated a one way service to Didcot Power Station, it has been recessed in the nearby Didcot yard until further work has been found. No. 58011 is seen stabled, in the Autumn of 1985 on the occasion of the GWS night photography event.

Christopher Lyons

Like all new traction and rolling stock, the Class 58s were subjected to extensive testing for a long period after their introduction. These two views show No. 58001 coupled to M&EE Test Car No. 6 (ADB975290) during the period performance testing was being carried out. Both views show the locomotive propelling the test car, which was taken from Derby to Derby via Branston Junction and Birmingham Curve Junction in order to turn its direction. The upper view shows the train approaching Burton, while the lower picture was taken near Stenson Junction.

Both: John Tuffs

Left & Left centre: In March 1985 a number of tests were carried out into the wheel slip/slide encountered with the Class 58s, for this programme numbers 58004/05 were monitored by M&EE Test Car No. 6 (ADB975290), which was coupled between the two locomotives. At first, light engine running was undertaken in the Derby, Nottingham and Sheffield area, but during the second week of the month the pair, complete with test car between operated the Ratcliffe – Fletton fly-ash train. The upper photograph shows Nos 58004/05 with test car between approaching Trowell Junction on 4th March, while the lower illustration shows the same pair, this time headed by No. 58005 near Peterborough on the fly-ash working. Note the mass of cables clipped to the cant rail of both locomotives.

John Tuffs/Les Nixon

Above right: Once the Class 58s commenced work in the Shirebrook area, West Burton and Cottam MGR duties soon became the regular stamping ground, displacing some Class 56s from the route. With a long 41 vehicle empty rake behind, No. 58003 is seen near Retford on 15th April 1987 bound for the Shirebrook area.

John Baker

Right: Both Cottam and West Burton Power Stations seem to have an insatiable thirst for coal, with some ten trains per day going to both destinations. No. 58004 is seen on the outskirts of Retford with an eastbound train.

John Baker

For many months after delivery the SEPEX Class 58 No. 58050 *Toton Traction Depot* was subjected to a rigorous test and evaluation programme based at Toton. This included operating selected trains and hauling, within the confines of Toton Depot, a line of ten withdrawn Class 45 locomotives. On 14th January 1988 No. 58050 is seen piloting sister No. 58005 with a long rake of empty mgr wagons at Stapleford, while en route to Bentinck Colliery.

John Tuffs

When in use on the Cottam and West Burton duties a number of locomotives are stabled in the Worksop area, and at weekends some eight examples could well be found. With another load of coal No. 58024 heads towards Retford from the Worksop direction in this April 1987 illustration.

John Baker

Storming away from Whisker Hill Junction, and heading towards Manton Colliery Junction No. 58024 takes its empty rake of HAA hoppers back to Shirebrook on 15th April 1987.

John Baker

Passing over yesteryears mode of freight transport – the canal, No. 58015 crosses a very low bridge over the barely navigable Chesterfield Canal near Manton on 20th August 1986 with a West Burton – Shirebrook Colliery empty MGR train.

Michael J. Collins

Fletton Fly-ash

One of the few non MGR duties diagrammed for a Class 58 is the daily Ratcliffe Power Station – Fletton fly-ash train, which provides a welcome break for Class 58 photographers. On 3rd June 1985 No. 58009 is seen arriving at Ratcliffe with empty hoppers from Fletton.

Gary Grafton

Between Ratcliffe and Syston Junction the fly-ash train traverses the slow lines, leaving the main lines clear for the regular IC125 services linking London with Derby, Sheffield and Nottingham. Class 58 No. 58013 is overtaken by an IC125 set with power car No. 43042 leading on the 17.20 St Pancras – Sheffield near Ratcliffe on 29th May 1986.

Michael J. Collins

The south bound loaded train departs Ratcliffe around noon, and takes some 90 minutes to reach Fletton. After same heavy snow No. 58007 passes Sutton Bonington near Kegworth while bound for Fletton on 25th January 1984. Note the unusual reflection in the cab windscreens.

John Tuffs

The fly-ash is transported in 21 tonne CSA type 'Presflo' wagons, constructed by BR at Ashford during the mid 1960s. The Fletton service is usually formed of around 40-45 vehicles, and on 5th November 1986 No. 58016 is seen at Barrow-on-Soar with the Fletton bound train.

Colin J. Marsden

Until 1960 the village of Hathern, to the north of Loughborough had a station, but today little trace remains. With Hathern offices behind, No. 58002 passes the village with the Ratcliffe – Fletton working on 6th December 1983.

John Tuffs

On a crisp and sunny 15th January 1984, No. 58007 storms towards Loughborough with the Fletton service, while on the north bound slow line a Corby – Lackenby 'Steeliner' can be seen, and in the far distance an IC125 approaches with a London bound service.

John Tuffs

In far from perfect weather conditions No. 58004 approaches Loughborough with the northbound empty service in July 1984. This train is operated by Toton crews throughout, so the return working is often well up to time, as once the crew has detached the wagons at Ratcliffe, they return to Toton light, and can go home.

Colin J. Marsden

After traversing the Midland Main Line as far south as Syston Junction, the fly-ash train bears left and takes the route via Melton Mowbray and Stamford to reach Peterborough. Displaying its 'Railfreight' plate on the front No. 58042 *Ironbridge Power Station* approaches Frisby on the Wreake with the 11.50 Ratcliffe – Fletton on 7th October 1986.

John Tuffs

When this illustration was taken on 3rd April 1984, locomotive No. 58011 was the latest example in traffic, departing from Doncaster in mid March. The Ratcliffe – Fletton train is seen near Melton Mowbray.

John Baker

Between Saxby and Oakham lays the village of Ashwell, which today is devoid of a station, the amenity having closed on 6th June 1966. No. 58018 is seen near Ashwell with the 15.35 Fletton – Ratcliffe empties on 20th May 1985.

John Baker

With the famous mud stains on the front end, caused by wheel splashes being quite apparent, No. 58004 passes Kirby Bellars near Melton Mowbray with the loaded train on 17th April 1984.

Michael J. Collins

With a mixture of colour light and semaphore signals being evident, No. 58013 passes Oakham station with the 15.35 Fletton – Ratcliffe (6M46) working of 30th May 1985. On the right of the picture there is evidence of signalling modernisation with a new pre-formed S&T hut and concrete cable troughing being present.

John Tuffs

Top: When working the fly-ash duties the Class 58s pass through some very pleasant countryside. Whilst the majority is comparatively flat this provides a good challenge to the photographer, and passing through the tranquil countryside near Oakham, No. 58018 heads for Fletton on 20th May 1987.

John Baker

Above: One of the benefits of going out to capture the fly-ash is the knowledge that the locomotive operating the morning loaded service to Fletton should, baring a failure, return with the afternoon empties, enabling the photographer to stake out his location and then just sit and wait. On 25th August 1985 No. 58011 is seen near Uffington with the empties bound for Ratcliffe.

John Baker

Left: Between Helpston and Peterborough the Melton Mowbray line travels alongside the ECML. Just south of Helpston near Woodcroft No. 58011 is seen with the Fletton bound train on 24th February 1984, the ECML tracks being on the right.

Colin J. Marsden

In flat countryside some very pleasing 'trains in the landscape' pictures can be obtained with a little thought. This view, looking across the fields near Woodcroft, shows No. 58004 heading for Peterborough, and gives a pleasing result with the telegraph poles adding required height to the picture.

John Baker

Although running adjacent to the ECML very few illustrations show the fly-ash train with an East Coast service. In pristine condition No. 58015 is seen on 24th July 1985 near Werrington with train 6E54, the 11.50 Ratcliffe CEGB – Fletton.

John Tuffs

Usually the Ratcliffe – Fletton train operates as a block train consist, however if any defect occurs or additional vehicles are needed at Fletton, shunting takes place adjacent to Peterborough station, usually with the empty train. On 13th October 1984 No. 58016 is seen shunting prior to returning to Ratcliffe.

John Baker

To enter the Fletton discharge terminal the trains head south from Peterborough to Fletton Junction where a spur goes into the unloading circuit. With several inches of snow laying No. 58022 heads for the terminal in January 1985.

Michael J. Collins

The Fletton terminal is arranged as a loop, thus avoiding the need to run round the train prior to returning to Ratcliffe. Prior to discharging its cargo No. 58002 creeps through the complex on 31st March 1984.

Ken Carr

The fly-ash which is generated at CEGB Ratcliffe Power Station is used for landfill purposes at Fletton, following the extraction of clay for the manufacture of bricks. During the annual Christmas double heading, Nos 58016/09 arrive at Fletton on 27th December 1984 with train No 6E54.

John Rudd

The sizeable North Nottinghamshire NCB area is looked after by Shirebrook depot, which has a sizeable number of footplate staff and uses a 'dedicated' Class 58 fleet. Passing Shirebrook depot on the left, containing various Class 56 and 58 locomotives, No. 58042 *Ironbridge Power Station* heads a Shirebrook Colliery – West Burton duty on 18th September 1987.

Colin J. Marsden

The Class 58s did not become common in the Shirebrook area until 1986, however various trains prior to this were recorded 58 hauled. On a bitterly cold 20th February 1986 No. 58007 is seen just north of the closed Shirebrook station with an MGR duty from the nearby Shirebrook Colliery.

John Tuffs

With the single line lead to Warsop Junction diverging to the right, No. 58036 heads towards Shirebrook station through the deep rock cutting, while hauling empty HAA wagons from West Burton to Shirebrook Colliery on 18th September 1987.

Colin J. Marsden

Heading for one of the Nottinghamshire pits, No. 58025 slowly traverses the single line Warsop Junction spur at Shirebrook on a bright 24th October 1985.

John Tuffs

With the track looking in far from a healthy state No. 58025 makes slow headway through Shirebrook Colliery after loading on 24th October 1985: The arched building ahead of the locomotive is one of the coal loading hoppers.

John Tuffs

The Class 58s have been requested at a number of depot open days, and on most occasions a member has been provided, although in some cases a rather dirty example has been produced. Looking far from clean, No. 58003 attended Cardiff Canton open day on 6th July 1985 and is seen in company with ex Class 24 departmental locomotive No. 97201.

Colin J. Marsden

For several years when the Midland Railway Centre at Butterley has held their major open days, Toton depot has provided a Class 58 for display. On 12-13th July 1986 when a special diesel event was held the latest example released from Doncaster, No. 58043 was loaned for the weekend, and is seen in company with Class 20 No. 20163 posed by the Butterley station name.

Colin J. Marsden

The only BR 'traffic' locomotive displayed at BREL Wolverton Works open day of 17th August 1985 was Class 58 No. 58026 which was neither cleaned for the event nor put on display in the main part of the works. No. 58026 is seen alongside the replica *Sans Pareil* steam locomotive.

Colin J. Marsden

Over the weekend of 2nd-3rd May 1986 a 'Mini Rail Weekend' was held at BREL Doncaster, the main exhibits being posed outside the paintshop. The latest Class 58 completed, No. 58042 was exhibited along with other traction old and new. This view of the paintshop yard shows from left to right No. 4771 *Green Arrow,* Nos 56007, 31184, D9000, and 58042.

Colin J. Marsden

The launch of the new 'Railfreight' dedicated locomotive liveries and logos was unveiled at Ripple Lane on Thursday 15th October 1987, when locomotives of all the major freight classes were represented, outshopped in the distinctive double grey livery. With its coal sector logo on the side No. 58050 *Toton Traction Depot* is seen in the yard at Ripple Lane.

Colin J. Marsden

On the Saturday following the Railfreight launch at Ripple Lane, a public open-day was held and a varied selection of motive power was made available for inspection. One of the most important visitors was of course No. 58050 which is seen in company with Class 37 No. 37892, Class 56 No. 56001, Class 47 No. 47079 and Class 59 No. 59001.

Colin J. Marsden

The only booked work for the Class 58s on the Southern Region is at the head of the Northfleet MGR duties, which number only two per day and even these operate on a rather infrequent basis. No. 58005 is seen in third rail territory at Lewisham on 3rd July 1986 at the head of a Silverhill Colliery – Northfleet duty.

Brian Beer

The Northfleet MGR duties are booked to use the Mid-Kent line to Dartford, however due to engineering work at Lewisham in August 1986, all services were diverted via the North Kent route taking Class 58s over this route for the first time. On 29th August 1986 No. 58012 is seen passing Plumstead with an additional Northfleet – Toton working.

Brian Beer

Between October 1987 and January 1988 the daily Didcot – Chessington 'Speedlink' coal train, which was diagrammed for a Class 37 locomotive, often produced a Class 58. On 23rd October 1987 No. 58022 passes through Wimbledon West Junction with the 10.20 service from Didcot. In the background Class 455/9 can be seen.

Colin J. Marsden

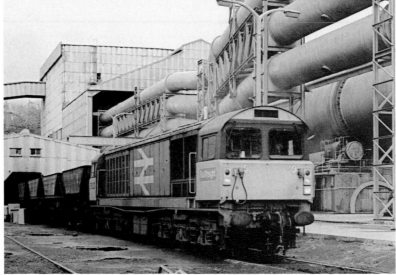

Dwarfed by the massive plant pipework, No. 58023 passes slowly through the discharge hopper at Blue Circle's Northfleet cement works on 11th November 1986 while in charge of an MGR working from Silverhill Colliery.

Keith Dungate

One of the first Class 58s to venture onto the Southern was on 16th July 1984 when No. 58014 hauled a Class 56 from Saltley to the SR for driver training, and then returned to the Midlands with a failed locomotive. No. 58014 is seen at Basingstoke station prior to collecting the failed locomotive from the yard.

Andrew French

The line between Knighton South Junction (Leicester) and Birmingham Curve Junction (Burton) sees a considerable amount of Class 58 activity, mainly in the form of MGR trains with operations being centred on Coalville. Taking the Drakelow line at Drakelow East Curve Junction No. 58002 painted in the new coal sub-sector livery heads trip from Coalville to Drakelow CEGB on 26th February 1988.

John Tuffs

Drakelow Power Station at the Burton end of the line receives a small number of trains each day, which are usually either Class 56 or 58 operated. On 29th August 1985 No. 58023 shunts HAA hoppers in the power station sidings. The intensity of the halogen headlight on the Class 58s is quite apparent from this illustration.

Michael J. Collins

Most of the coal for Drakelow Power Station emulates from one of the nearby pits. This has considerable advantage with manpower and one driver is quite able to operate two trains during his shift, productivity in this field was increased when flexible rostering was introduced, enabling a man to be diagrammed for up to nine hours per shift. On 21st March 1986 No. 58028 passes the site of Gresley station with a Coalfields Farm – Drakelow trip.

John Tuffs

With the towers of Drakelow Power Station just visible in the distance No. 58029 is seen near Gresley on 10th October 1986 with a Drakelow CEGB – Mantle Lane (Coalville) empty HAA/HDA formation.

John Tuffs

Considerable subsidence has occurred near Moira West, where underground NCB excavations have caused the track to drop some five feet, although the railway have tried in vain to stop the movement, little improvement has been recorded. Passing over the subsided area No. 58010 heads for Moira West on 2nd October 1985 with a Drakelow – Bagworth working.

John Tuffs

Opposite Moira West signal box is the line to Rawdon Colliery, which sees an amount of Class 58 activity. Operating under its slow speed mode, while loading was being effected No. 58040 creeps towards the exit signal with an export coal train bound for Garston Docks on 10th July 1986.
Colin J. Marsden

As the shunter gives the 'ease couplings' handsignal, the driver of No. 58005 applies power to slacken the coupling on a rake of HAA hoppers which are to be stabled in Overseal sidings, in readiness for their next duty. Note the unofficial position of the tail lamp being carried.
John Tuffs

To the east of Coalville is the aptly named Coalfields Farm opencast site, which generates about six trains per day, depending on coalface output. On 11th September 1985 production had been sufficient to fill some 32 HAA wagons forming a Didcot CEGB working which was captured on film approaching Coalville, headed by No. 58025.

John Tuffs

With the now demolished Coalville signal box dominating the background, No. 58025 heads for Coalfields Farm with a rake of empty HAA hoppers on 11th September 1985. Whilst operating on the Leicester – Burton line most locomotives are stabled at Coalville, which also hosts the local train crew signing-on point.

John Tuffs

Another colliery loader situated on the Coalville line is Bagworth, although the actual working face is some miles away. After loading 41 HAA wagons No. 58027 slowly moves to the exit signal to gain the 'main' line with another load of coal bound for Drakelow CEGB Power Station.

John Tuffs

Although owned by 'Railfreight' few Class 58s ever operate general air braked freight traffic. With the sizeable yards of Washwood Heath behind, No. 58005 heads a mixture of British and Continental air braked stock on the 11.00 Banbury – Bescot AB5 of 5th February 1985.

Colin J. Marsden

Undoubtedly deputising for the booked motive power No. 58008 is seen near Saxby between Oakham and Melton Mowbray on 17th April 1984 with the 11.00 Corby – Toton 'Air Brake Network' feeder service. The train being formed of a privately owned scrap steel carrier, and 14 open steel wagons which were all sheeted.

Michael J. Collins

Without doubt the most infamous air brake freight ever entrusted to a Class 58 was the daily Toton – Arpley (as far as Ashburys), and return service, which in 1984-5 was a Class 58 booking. On 19th October 1984 No. 58014 is seen near Trowell Junction with the Toton bound service.

John Tuffs

No. 58011 is shown traversing the up slow line between Tapton Junction and Chesterfield on 21st February 1985 with the Ashburys – Toton service, on this occasion formed of one VTG tank wagon and four 'Railfreight' box vehicles.

Colin J. Marsden

Using little of its 60,000 lb tractive effort to lift its 130 tonne freight, No. 58022 passes Trowell Junction on the down main line on 19th February 1985 with the 08.43 Toton – Warrington (to Ashburys) working.

Colin J. Marsden

The Ashburys bound ABS departed from Toton in an up direction, travelling via Beeston, and Lenton Junctions to emerge on the Midland main line heading north at Trowell Junction. The north bound service of 22nd February 1985 is seen approaching Lenton South Junction headed by No. 58022.

Colin J. Marsden

With its usual lightweight load, which eventually led to the withdrawal of the service, No. 58009 passes the site of the former Ilkeston Junction station on 18th February 1985 while in charge of the 12.46 Ashburys – Toton (7M60).

Colin J. Marsden

With two other intrepid Class 58 photographers, Messrs Gater and Tuffs, the author waited over two hours in sub zero temperature for the return Ashburys freight on 19th February 1985, however all were rewarded with this view of No. 58022 with just three vans! Seen passing Shipley Gate.

Colin J. Marsden

Some four miles south of Chesterfield is Clay Cross Junction where the Sheffield – Derby and Nottingham lines part company. Passing the site of the former Clay Cross station No. 58019 powers the 12.46 Ashburys – Toton on 15th March 1985. The first two wagons behind the locomotive are carrying wheelsets for attention at Derby works.

John Tuffs

Hauling the ultimate freight train of just one wagon No. 58002 heads the 6F52 10.00 Corby – Toton air braked freight past Kegworth on 10th April 1984. At the time the working was used for driver training, however little brake training could be achieved with this load!

John Tuffs

Prior to being named *Cottam Power Station* No. 58040 departs from Toton yard near Long Eaton Town on 25th June 1986 with the 7G82, 10.05 'Speedlink' from Toton Old Bank to Bescot. The train is formed primarily of coal wagons of the HBA type with two VDA vans in the middle.

John Tuffs

There have been very few occasions that Class 58s have been recorded hauling oil trains, however this illustration of No. 58005 passing Burton on 29th August 1985 has come to light, but regrettably the photographer was unable to identify the actual train.
Michael J. Collins

Passing Branston Junction, south of Burton No. 58037 is seen at the head of empty bitumen tanks on 18th July 1986 forming the 20.35 Mantle Lane (Coalville) – Stanlow North. The line diverging in the background is that to Drakelow and Coalville.
John Tuffs

No. 58004 passes Leicester Junction, Burton on 25th May 1984 while heading the 21.25 (TTho) Ellesmere Port – Bardon Hill bitumen tanks. This train is rather unusual to photograph in action as it is booked to arrive overnight, however on the day this photograph was taken the line to Bardon Hill had been closed, and the train stabled overnight near Burton.

John Tuffs

On a very murky 21st February 1985 No. 58022 is seen traversing the north bound slow line at Chesterfield with an unidentified ABS bound for Doncaster. The train consisted of a BR VCA van, two privately owned scrap steel carriers, five BDAs loaded with sleepers, and eight motorail flats carrying Ford vehicles.

Colin J. Marsden

To provide drivers with a 'train' to handle during their Class 58 conversion course, a fleet of 'Railfreight' HBA wagons were set aside in the Birmingham area in Autumn 1984 when driver training was a weekly occurrence. No. 58004 is seen descending Hatton Bank on 23rd August while en route for Oxford.

John Tuffs

At a number of public events, 'Railfreight' have provided exhibition formations of modern freight stock. One of the most interesting was at Coalville where Class 58 No. 58023 was provided to shunt up and down a siding on 31st August 1985 with 15 different vehicle types, from both the BR and private sector fleets.

John Tuffs

Following an 'on line' failure No. 58034 *Basset-law* is seen piloting Class 45/0 No. 45046 with a rake of ICI chemical tanks through Barton and Walton, Staffordshire on 9th May 1987. The train was identified as the 05.40 Stoke Gifford – Scunthorpe West (6E41), which was running very late.

John Tuffs

Obviously due to the failure of the Class 47 train engine, No. 58011 is seen hauling a Broughton Lane bound BOC train at Woodburn Junction on the outskirts of Sheffield during October 1984. The Class 47s are not fitted with any multiple operating facility so if these two types were to be operated together under normal conditions a driver would be required on each locomotive.

Les Nixon

It is not every day that Class 58s are observed passing Doncaster on anything but MGR duties, however on 13th August 1985 the photographer was lucky enough to capture No. 58016 heading south with a freight that had emulated in the Scunthorpe area.

Les Nixon

A new air braked 'Speedlink' freight service commenced operation in 1986 between Melton Mowbray and Ardwick, conveying pet food from the nearby Pedigree plant. The train is usually diagrammed for a Class 47 or 56, however on 11th September 1987 No. 58009 was rostered for the duty and is seen passing Clay Cross.

John Tuffs

With the headquarters of Brush Electrical Engineering behind, No. 58004 passes Loughborough on 21st December 1983 with the 11.00 Corby – Toton sheeted steel train. At the time this illustration was taken the duty was used for crew training.

John Tuffs

Around Toton

Around Toton, the Class 58s home location is one of their major operating areas, and if photographers are trying to find examples of the class at work, they are best advised to try this locality. At the south of Toton is Long Eaton Town, where No. 58009 is seen approaching, on 20th February 1985 with an MGR train for Castle Donington Power Station.

Colin J. Marsden

With the huge Toton yards on either side No. 58003 storms through on the main line with a Ratcliffe bound MGR on 29th May 1985. The two tracks on the right diverge from the main line and form the high level line to Meadow Lane Junction and either Trent Junction or the Attenborough line.

Michael J. Collins

Approaching Toton at the south end from Meadow Lane Junction No. 58007 brings in an empty rake of HAA wagons from Ratcliffe Power Station on 3rd March 1986. This route into Toton is used by most services that are booked into the yard, thus avoiding any congestion on the main line.

John Tuffs

As Toton is the major train crew depot in the area it is quite usual for trains to be recessed in one of the reception roads whilst a change of driver/guard is carried out. With clouds of exhaust, identifying that the machine had been left idling for a lengthy period No. 58029 departs south from Toton with a Garston working on 3rd March 1986.

John Tuffs

At the north end of Toton is Sandiacre, where there was a station until January 1967, and is the start of the Erewash Valley line. No. 58036 shunts empty MGR hoppers into Toton yard off a Willington working on 5th November 1986. At the rear of the MGR train is the rail entrance to Toton depot.

Colin J. Marsden

Traversing the up main line at Stapleford and Sandiacre indicating that the train is unlikely to stop for a crew change, No. 58037 heads a 41 vehicle rake of HAA/HDA wagons on 5th November 1986 with trip 7T50 from Silverhill to Castle Donington.

Colin J. Marsden

With the rear of the train just clearing Milford Tunnel, No. 58041 approaches Duffield with a Renishaw Park (near Barrow Hill) – Willington MGR working on 1st April 1986. The locomotive was in pristine condition having been released from Doncaster Works eight days before.

John Tuffs

There are few MGR trains that traverse the Midland Main Line south of Trent, one exception being the infrequent Northfleet workings. On 2nd May 1986 No. 58010 is seen at Normanton-on-Soar with the 13.23 Toton New Bank – Northfleet working.

Jean W. Marsden

Left: Instead of travelling via Leicester, the Northfleet duties travel via Syston, Manton and Corby, thus avoiding the Leicester area. On 15th August 1986 No. 58040 is illustrated near Kirby Bellars with the 09.29 Silverhill – Northfleet duty.

John Tuffs

Right: A 58 under the wires! For just over ten miles between Lichfield and Rugeley the Class 58s operate under the LM overhead wires, to gain access to Rugeley CEGB Power Station, which normally receives some 3-4 trains per day from the Coalville area. On 10th May 1985 No. 58004 is seen passing through Rugeley station with the 16.42 Bagworth – Rugeley, train No. 7G23.

John Tuffs

Right, bottom: Passing the beautiful Midland Railway signal box at Dudding Hill, No. 58037 traverses the freight only line between Cricklewood and Acton Wells Junction with a Silverhill Colliery – Northfleet working on 23rd July 1986.

Brian Beer

Below: Traversing the now freight only line between Wichnor Junction and Lichfield Trent Valley, No. 58031 passes the village of Alrewas on 8th October 1985 with the 09.07 Bagworth – Rugeley CEGB working.

John Tuffs

As previously illustrated the first appearance of a Class 58 in the London Division of the WR was on 3rd May 1984 when No. 58014 operated light locomotive to Old Oak Common for training purposes. At just before mid-day the locomotive hauling nine Mk II FOs departed for Oxford, the train being seen passing West Ealing on the down main line.

Colin J. Marsden

The first occasion that a Class 58 operated on passenger stock was on 21st April 1983 when No. 58001 hauled eleven Mk II vehicles from Doncaster to Peterborough and return, in conjunction with test purposes. The train is seen departing from Peterborough at 15.12 on its return journey to Doncaster.

Ian Cowley

During the second week of May No. 58014 made several crew training runs on the WR main line between Old Oak Common and Oxford, one of these is seen approaching Reading on 7th May, again with the FO rake.

Colin J. Marsden

Probably the most publicised Class 58 passenger working was on 1st September 1984 when No. 58002 hauled a failed IC125 on the 12.10 Liverpool – Penzance forward from Birmingham all the way to Plymouth! Making Western Region history No. 58002 pulls the delinquent set out of Totnes, running some 45 minutes late.

Peter Green

After the diagrammed locomotive had suffered a failure No. 58024 was utilised to haul the 14.00 Euston – Shrewsbury forward from Birmingham on 9th June 1985. This illustration shows the locomotive waiting with the empty stock to return to Oxley carriage sidings, from where the locomotive returned light to Bescot.

Mark Lawrence

On 20th September 1986 Hertfordshire Railtours operated the "Lincolnshire Coast Pullman" railtour from London King's Cross to Cleethorpes and Skegness, powered by a Class 58 throughout. Recently named No. 58039 *Rugeley Power Station* was diagrammed, being the first Class 58 into King's Cross. The train is seen in King's Cross just prior to departure.

Colin J. Marsden

The stock used for the tour was the Bounds Green maintained 'Pullman Rail' set, which made a most interesting contrast behind the 'Railfreight' liveried Class 58. The train is seen at Skegness prior to shunting out of the station and run round to make the journey via Doncaster to Cleethorpes.

Colin J. Marsden

The return working from Cleethorpes was via Doncaster, Mexborough and Worksop, regaining the ECML at Retford. This night illustration shows the train at Stevenage, the final setting down point before King's Cross.

Albert Dawson

Making the unusual appearance of a 'Railfreight' locomotive in King's Cross *Rugeley Power Station* rests at the buffers after its 500+ mile round trip, before returning light locomotive to Doncaster.

Colin J. Marsden

Severnside Railtours chartered a Class 58 on 15th July 1984 to power part of the journey of their "South Yorkshireman" tour from Cardiff to Cleethorpes. In this illustration the train is seen at Whitacre Junction near Water Orton, motive power being provided by No. 58014.

John Tuffs

124

The ''South Yorkshireman'' was Class 58 powered between Birmingham and Sheffield and return as only a limited number of train crews had been trained on their operation at the time. The return leg of the tour is seen passing Peartree near Derby.

John Tuffs

The use of Class 58s or any air brake only motive power on railtours can cause operating problems, as only air braked rolling stock can be used, and this is usually in much demand. On 16th September 1984 Hertfordshire Railtours operated their ''Midland Macedoine'' tour from St Pancras to Buxton and return, which used No. 58007 for part of the journey. In this view the train is seen near Spondon en route for Buxton.

John Tuffs

With the freight only line to Peak Forest disappearing to the left behind the locomotive, No. 58007 shunts the "Midland Macedoine" railtour at Buxton during the evening of 16th September 1984.

Les Nixon

With a 'Boris the Basher' headboard on the front lamp iron No. 58012 powers the Railway Enthusiasts Society Limited's "The South Yorkshireman III" tour from London Victoria to Doncaster on 24th March 1985. The train is seen passing Lichfield Trent Valley Junction on the outward section of the tour.

John Tuffs

With the location of the former Overseal sidings behind the locomotive No. 58018 passes Moira West signal box with the F&W railtours "Coalville Slug" charter of 1st September 1985. When this illustration was taken the train was on the Coalville – Matlock section of the tour.

John Tuffs

With plenty of 'haulage bashers' hanging from the windows, the F&W "Coalville Slug" tour is seen emerging from Holt Lane Tunnel, Matlock with the return charter bound for Penzance – still with No. 58018 providing the power.

Peter Gater

On 29th June 1986 No. 58008 is seen speeding through Shipley Gate, on the Erewash Valley line with the return leg of the F&W the "Plant Pursuer" railtour which had eminated from Plymouth and visited Doncaster Works after travelling over various lines in the East Midlands, including the Lincoln avoiding line. The Class 58 was replaced at Toton by Class 47 No. 47432.

John Tuffs

The very first passenger carrying train hauled by a Class 58 was the "58 Pioneer" tour from Paddington to Matlock on 18th September 1983, for which No. 58002 performed the honours between Nuneaton and Matlock via Nottingham. The train is seen departing from Nottingham in this illustration.

Les Nixon